MOTO GUZZI

FORZA IN MOVIMENTO

DAVID G. STYLES

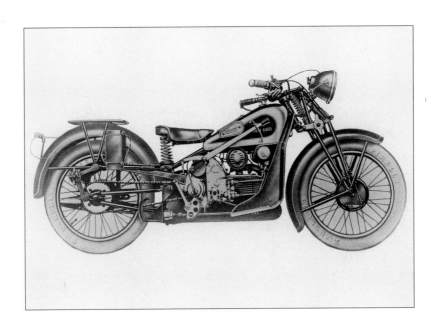

SUTTON PUBLISHING

Sutton Publishing Limited
Phoenix Mill . Thrupp . Stroud
Gloucestershire . GL5 2BU

First published 2000

British Library Cataloguing in Publication Data
A catalogue record for this book is available from the British Library.

ISBN 0-7509-2041-6

Title page photograph: a 1930 GT2VT, one of Moto Guzzi's first saddle-tanked motor cycles. Truly a Grand Tourer.

ACKNOWLEDGEMENTS

Illustrations in this book have been sourced from, and are reproduced by kind permission of, Moto Guzzi Sport and the author.

Dedication

To my wife Ann, my daughter Emma
and my son Philip
who continue to indulge me in my writings.

Typeset in 10.5/13.5 Photina.
Typesetting and origination by
Sutton Publishing Limited.
Printed and bound in England by
J.H. Haynes and Co. Ltd, Sparkford.

CONTENTS

CHRONOLOGY

1920	The GP (Guzzi e Parodi) prototype motor cycle is completed
1921	Societa Anonima Moto Guzzi formed at Mandello del Lario
1921	Moto Guzzi's first race victory — the Targa Florio
1923	C2V wins Circuito del Lario on its debut: Sport Model launched
1924	C4V announced — wins Circuito del Lario and the European Championship
1926	Moto Guzzi 250 finishes second at Isle of Man TT — only to be disqualified over a plug change
1927	World's first true sprung-frame motor cycle announced — the GT
1928	Sport 14 announced, also Tipo 107, first Motocarro three-wheeler
1928	Moto Guzzi wins its first military order for 245 examples of the GT
1930	Quattro Cilindri — four-cylinder transverse-engined racer built
1932	Moto Guzzi enters lightweight market with P175
1932	Tre Cilindri 500 announced and GT17 supplied to armed forces
1933	Bicilindrica 500cc racer's debut at Italian GP — finishes second
1934	Bicilindrica wins Spanish and Italian GPs and Italian 500 Championship
1935	Stanley Woods wins 250cc and 500cc TTs — Moto Guzzi's first TT win
1935	Italy invades Ethiopia
1936	Giulio Cesare Carcano joins Moto Guzzi
1937	Omobono Tenni wins Isle of Man Lightweight TT on Albatros
1938	Condor 500 Single production racer/Ercolino Motocarro introduced
1939	Airone 250 production and Albatros 250 production racer launched
1940	Tre Cilindri supercharged 500cc racer built
1940	Italy enters the Second World War; Moto Guzzi builds Alce/Super Alce/Trialce in quantity for armed forces
1943	Italian realignment with Allies in the Second World War
1945	End of the Second World War
1946	New Moto Guzzi range includes Airone, GT, Motoleggera 65, Motocarro
1946	Return to amateur racing with Dondolino 500
1948	Maurice Cann wins Lightweight TT on Albatros 250
1948	Omobono Tenni dies at Swiss GP, Bremgarten, testing 250 parallel twin
1949	Introduction of Gambalunghino 250 racer
1950	Introduction of Galetto 150 and Falcone 500
1952	Quattro Cilindri (longitudinale) 500 built
1953	New 350cc and 500cc racing singles in Bialbero frame and Zigolo launched
1955	Otto Cilindri first and only V8-engined motor cycle built
1955	Death of Giorgio Parodi
1956	Launch of Lodola 175, Carlo Guzzi's last complete design
1957	Moto Guzzi withdraws from first-class racing
1960	Introduction of Stornello 125
1960	Giulio Carcano's V-Twin first appears in 3 x 3 'Mule' as 754cc
1963	Dingo 50cc introduces new lightweight to Guzzi range
1964	Carlo Guzzi dies aged seventy-five
1966	Introduction of Trotter 40cc moped
1967	Moto Guzzi goes into receivership/V7 big twin first launched as 704cc
1969	100km/1000km speed records in 750cc and 1000cc classes set at Monza
1971	V7 Sport, Nuovo Falcone and 850cc models announced

1972	Acquisition of Moto Guzzi by de Tomaso Industries
1972	First Le Mans model Moto Guzzi
1974	V1000-I Convert first automatic transmission Moto Guzzi
1974	125 Tuttoterreno/Turismo, 350/400GTS, 250TS, Cross and Nibbio launched
1976	254 transverse four launched
1977	V35 and V50 Series V-twins launched
1979	Introduction of V35 Imola
1981	V65 model range launched
1985	V75 model range launched, also 125C and 125TT models
1986	NTX Enduro-style models launched in V35, V65 and V75 versions
1987	California III, Mille GT/650GT/350GT models announced
1988	SP III and Le Mans V models launched
1989	750 Strada/SP/Targa/Nevada models launched
1990	750NTX police motor cycle first produced
1991	First production Daytona built, to go on sale in 1992
1992	Quota 1000 first produced
1993	Strada 1000/California 1000EV/California 1100 on sale
1994	1000 Sport IE/1100 Sport launched; Moto Guzzi reorganised
1996	Centauro/Centauro GT/Sport launched; Moto Guzzi 75th anniversary
1997	Tamarix Investors become the major shareholder in Moto Guzzi
1998	Quota 1100ES launched; the decision is made to move Moto Guzzi to Monza
1999	Monza move cancelled, further reorganisation; V11 Sport launched
2000	Moto Guzzi celebrates eight decades since the construction of the GP prototype

Now if you want a motor cycle with everything, try the 1989 California III with its dual shaped seats, rear seat backrest, side panniers and top box, full fairing and gold lining. If big cruisers are your thing, then this California takes a lot of beating. The model was introduced in 1987, but this later version has the more rounded luggage rack. Surprisingly, perhaps, it was capable of over 110mph.

Two of Italy's finest-engineered products of their time. When Benito Mussolini visited Reggio Calabria in 1938 he travelled in his favourite car, an Alfa Romeo 6c2500. More Alfas follow their leader while the outrider escorts are astride the other government favourite, Moto Guzzi GT20s. The riders are members of the Milizia della Strada. Mussolini took the view that manufacturers whose products had done well in competition deserved government support. Moto Guzzi and Alfa Romeo both had outstanding credentials in this area, so secured the business.

CHAPTER ONE

THREE MEN AND A MOTOR CYCLE

The brain behind the product – Carlo Guzzi, in his later years. This quite modest little man was fired with a burning ambition from his early youth to create an original and advanced motor bicycle. His first design was the product of a very close study of the design principles of bicycles and early single-cylinder engines. That first machine was a clear demonstration of Guzzi's capacity to learn and his thorough approach.

In the period before the First World War, it is most unlikely that members of the Italian families of Guzzi, Parodi and Ravelli would have crossed paths, let alone come together in business. Carlo Guzzi was born into a modest family situation in Milan in 1889. Even as a small boy he proved to be a natural mechanic, and as he grew up he took a keen interest in motor cycles. His family frequently took holidays in the small town of Mandello Tonzanico, where they owned a couple of small houses. The town was located at the foot of Mount Grigna, about 10 kilometres to the north of Lecco, on the eastern shore of Lake Como, and and it was here that young Carlo came to know the local blacksmith Giorgio Ripamonti, who introduced him to the mysteries of the internal combustion engine. It was during this period that Carlo Guzzi began to gather together the design ideas for his first motor cycle.

Giorgio Parodi was born in Genoa into a well-to-do family, who were ship-owners and manufacturers in the naval armaments industry. The family was established in the old traditions of Italian society; and Giorgio's father Emanuele was head of the family dynasty. Before the war there was little likelihood of links being forged between men of such contrasting backgrounds but times were changing, and the way in which Guzzi and Parodi met was a sign of those changes.

Giovanni Ravelli was born into a wealthy family in Brescia (a town later renowned for its position on the route of the Mille Miglia – the most famous motor race in history). Like Carlo Guzzi, young Giovanni had discovered an affinity with motor cycles; because he could afford to indulge his growing passion, he rode motor cycles in competition. He achieved success in his chosen sport and became one of the most noted racers in pre-war Italy.

These three young men came together as a result of Italy's involvement in that war. Certainly the social order changed after the war but it was not entirely the result of the mould being broken by the 'deprived classes'. Many young members of the nobility and gentry welcomed the social changes taking place after their experiences in the war, when men of all classes and backgrounds had been thrown together in battle, sharing the powerful sense of interdependence that results only from having a common cause – survival. This closeness was particularly apparent in the newly formed flying services, and these three young men found themselves in the Italian Air Corps. When Italy entered the war in 1915, Carlo Guzzi was conscripted into the army, while Giorgio Parodi and Giovanni Ravelli volunteered to join the infant Air Corps as pilots. Guzzi, in the meantime, had discovered the existence of this elite corps and his natural mechanical skills helped him to obtain a transfer from the infantry.

By chance Guzzi, Parodi and Ravelli found themselves serving with the same squadron. Carlo Guzzi was a good technician, his familiarity with motor cycle engines transferring easily to the rotary aero engines of the day. He and Giovanni Ravelli soon discovered their common interest and, in those changing circumstances of war, the barriers of class and rank were lowered and the two became friends. As pilots, Ravelli and Giorgio Parodi also became friends and no doubt Parodi was frequently bombarded with Ravelli's passion for motor cycles. Guzzi's great skill in keeping flying machines operating reliably and the interests he shared with Ravelli meant that the three men soon came together and began discussing their plans for after the war. Giorgio Parodi became involved in the business aspect of Carlo Guzzi's motor cycle designs while Giovanni Ravelli was keen to ride them. So the three formed a pact: they would go into business together after the war and manufacture motor cycles. Giorgio Parodi was confident he could persuade his father to take an interest and so raise the capital essential to form the company and, more importantly, to construct their first motor cycle.

Shortly after the start of Italy's involvement in the war Carlo Guzzi's mother had moved to Mandello, now renamed Mandello del Lario, and when Carlo was discharged from the Air Corps it was to Mandello del Lario that he went, and it was there that the fledgling company would be formed. Sadly, however, the trio could never realise their dream; even though all three had survived the rigours of war, Giovanni Ravelli was killed in a flying accident late in 1918. His death left the new company without its star rider and a key partner, but Giorgio Parodi fulfilled his promise and approached his father for help to get the new company off the ground. Emanuele Parodi would doubtless have found it odd that Giorgio wanted to go into partnership with an enlisted man, but he trusted his son's judgement, and when he met young Carlo there was an instant affinity between the two men, and Emanuele soon produced the 2,000 Lire needed to construct that first machine.

Guzzi's prototype machine had many novel features. For example, the engine was mounted horizontally, not in the upright position used on many motor cycles of the time, and more significantly the gearbox was in unit with the engine – a pioneering concept. The prototype had a single overhead camshaft and four valves closed by hairpin-type springs – four valves are all the rage in modern motor cycles, but it was another novel idea at this time. The engine also enjoyed dual ignition, the sparks being provided by a Bosch magneto. The bore and stroke were unusual for the time, too, with oversquare dimensions of 88 x 82mm. Because the engine was so low slung, the centre of gravity was also low, allowing the lower longitudinal tube of the frame (on which was mounted the fuel tank), to be positioned below the normal level; it also facilitated the sloping of the top tube, above the fuel tank, to allow a low seating position.

The frame of the prototype had two downtubes from the headstock, passing one each side of the cylinder head and cradling the engine/gearbox unit. There was no front wheel brake on this machine, but the single drum back brake had four shoes inside, operated by two cams, one by means of a left foot pedal, the other by the right hand from a lever on the handlebars. This novel machine was presented to Emanuele Parodi for his inspection. Parodi had already looked closely at the market-place at large and had 'checked out' Carlo Guzzi to his satisfaction. Now he had to decide whether the machine Guzzi had produced was worth further investment. It was – and Parodi made money available to implement the manufacture of machines for sale.

That first machine was known as the 'GP' (Guzzi e Parodi). Completed in 1920, it had a few non-Italian components, including a British carburetter (an AMAC semi-automatic slide type) and British Dunlop 26 x 2½in tyres. The manufacturing workshops were established across the road from Mandello del Lario's railway station, and so impressed was Emanuele Parodi with Guzzi's skills that he recommended 'Moto Guzzi' as the name of the new company. This was adopted and, after some discussion, the young partnership of Carlo Guzzi and Giorgio Parodi settled on a badge for the new company. To commemorate their lost friend Giovanni Ravelli, they decided to adopt the eagle emblem of the Italian Air Corps, placing the name in sans serif block capitals below the eagle. Thus, in 1920, was born Italy's oldest surviving motor cycle manufacturer and one of the industry's greatest names.

The initial funding for the prototype, and his continuing support for the business as it became established, meant that Emanuele Vittorio Parodi was thoroughly committed to the success of Moto Guzzi. His business training and natural abilities were a great asset to the company, and his forthrightness was one of the factors in the company's reputation. Straight dealing, high quality and sporting achievement were the three key ingredients in the legend of Moto Guzzi, and Emanuele Parodi was chairman of the company from its incorporation as Societa Anonima Moto Guzzi on 21 March 1921 until his death.

However, Emanuele Vittorio Parodi was a careful man and a key reason for his insistence that the company be named Moto Guzzi and not GP was that these initials were also those of his son Giorgio, and he would not want that association to be made if the business failed. On the other hand, it is interesting to note that Carlo Guzzi never had shares in the company that bore his name: all the shares in the newly formed company were held by Signor Parodi and instead Carlo Guzzi was paid a royalty on every machine that left the factory. Of course, there was some advantage in this for Guzzi, since he would carry none of the financial responsibilities if the company failed, but the likelihood of that happening was slim.

Guzzi's prototype was not, however, to be Moto Guzzi's first production model because Carlo and his partner quickly realised that it would be far too expensive to manufacture and thus very difficult to sell in any numbers. Furthermore, a four-valve twin-cam engine would not be simple to maintain – in those days there was no service network for motor cycles! Consequently they went back to the drawing-board to design an engine that would be much cheaper to produce in quantity and much easier for its owner to maintain, at a time when maintenance was largely a matter of 'make-do-and-mend' after something had broken. The first production machine would be known as the 'Normale'.

Within twenty years Moto Guzzi's origins as a small workshop manufacturing motor cycles had grown into one of the most important organisations in its industry. The reliability of the Mandello machines, combined with the tremendous publicity they earned from their competition successes, brought them to the notice of Il Duce, Benito Mussolini, the leader of Italy's pre-war Fascist government. As a result motor cycles, mostly Moto Guzzis, were built by the thousand for military and public authority use. Two- and three-wheeled machines were built for the armed forces, the police authorities and public utilities, as well as for the general public. Then, after the war, the company started to produce much smaller motor cycles, such as the 65cc Motoleggera, to meet the demands of a much-changed market.

As you walk through the Mandello del Lario factory today, you have a sense of timelessness, in that the dedication and commitment to quality that created Moto Guzzi's early reputation lingers there still. You can watch the machining of metals into machine parts, the checking and assembly of engines and gearboxes, the bringing together of all the components that make up a motor cycle, then the final assembly of the motor cycles themselves. And then there's the test track, where Moto Guzzis are given a brief track test around the factory site before final inspection and pass off. The motor cycles built today are just as much state of the art as they ever were and at times you can almost sense the spirit of Carlo Guzzi hovering around the factory he established eighty years ago. Occasionally at Mandello de Lario you may catch a glimpse of Umberto Todero, one of the engineering team responsible for creating the magnificent racing machines that led to Stanley Woods' TT victories before the Second World War and which formed the foundation of post-war racing successes. Moto Guzzi is truly the 'Eagle of Lake Como'.

Two-views of the Mandello del Lario factory where Italy's greatest motor-cycling legend has been built for almost eighty years. The model shows the layout of the whole plant, with the test-track running round the building at the left rear of the picture. The frontage does not face green fields, as the picture suggests, though. In fact, the car park opposite the plant ends at the railway embankment of Mandello station. The lower picture, taken early on a Sunday morning in July, shows the upper end of the frontage viewed from the car park. The buildings are well maintained but show none of the trappings of modern office blocks, such as air conditioning. They are an integral part of Mandello's modern industrial history and continue to be the home of Moto Guzzi.

Here's the car park just across the street from the factory and, beyond that, the railway station with one of the most famous names in motor-cycling – Mandello del Lario. If you travelled by train to Moto Guzzi, you would walk about a hundred metres to the front door from the station. The author never used the station, as he drove from Milan to Mandello each day during his visit, but a northern Italian train ride could be a fascinating part of 'the tour'.

Abbadia Lariana is the town before Mandello del Lario as you drive, or ride, along the coast road from Lecco. Such is the esteem in which Mandello's most famous son is held that the central square in this little town is named after him. The author, sitting in a traffic queue, took a quick visual check of his surroundings and spotted the name on the stone in the ivy at the back of the car park – 'Piazza Carlo Guzzi'.

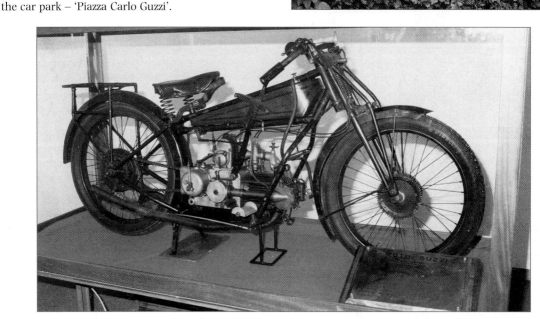

Carlo Guzzi's first creation brought many advanced features to the motor cycle, including the low centre of gravity, the in-unit engine and gearbox, the duplex frame and the low saddle position (some of which were still being declared as 'new' by other manufacturers thirty years later!). The four-valve engine set the pattern for Guzzi engine designs for years, while its horizontal position provided the best and most even cooling for the cylinder head. It's hardly surprising, then, that Emanuele Parodi decided to back his son Giorgio in this new venture.

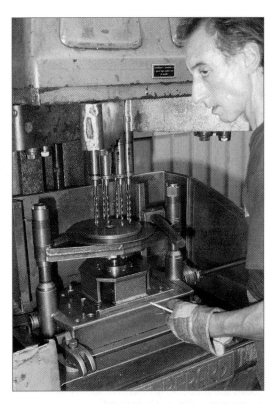

Meticulous care is taken at every stage of manufacture. The cylinder barrels are dipped prior to machine-finishing at Mandello, while the machine shop is clean and tidy and rigorously controlled to high quality standards. The deep sense of family loyalty among the workforce helps to maintain quality standards, as there are grandsons of founder workers to be found here.

In these two pictures we see small components and large units of motor cycles coming together. On the left, machine-finished camshafts sit in cages awaiting installation into engines; above, the beautifully finished fully assembled engines. The tags on these engines indicate that they have passed the bench run test and are ready for installation into motor cycles. Each engine is bench run after assembly and signed off as fit for use. This is Moto Guzzi today.

While engines are assembled in one part of the Mandello factory, frames come together in another. This one has just emerged from the paint booth and is receiving its fittings before it goes down the line for final assembly. The Moto Guzzi tracks are certainly not mass production lines, but they do allow the assembly of motor cycles in the time-honoured fashion of bringing components to the track and adding them progressively as the frame moves along; what starts as a barely fitted frame at one end of the track ends as a complete near-roadworthy Moto Guzzi at the other.

The finished machine, inspected at every stage of construction, has had its engine bench run and the frame checked, the running gear tested and the fittings examined. Now it's time for a track test. Guzzis are track tested within the factory site before being passed off for release to distributors worldwide.

CHAPTER TWO

SETTING TRENDS – FROM PROTOTYPE TO THE EARLY SINGLES

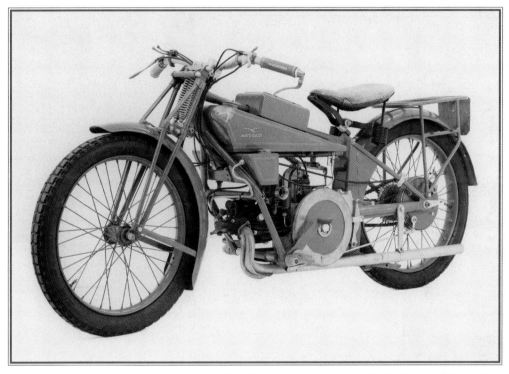

The first production Moto Guzzi was the Tipo Normale, launched in 1921. It was still a 500cc machine but the engine design was revised in order to keep manufacturing costs down. The original four-valve cylinder head, while a most efficient design, required more machining and assembly time than the overhead exhaust/side inlet concept adopted for the first catalogue model. The Normale quickly became a success and launched Moto Guzzi on the road to becoming an integral part of Italy's motor-cycling heritage.

Like most teenagers the world over, young Carlo Guzzi dreamed of fame and fortune. Unlike most teenagers, however, his dream was based on solid foundations. His fame and fortune would come from creating the most advanced and best-built motor cycle in Italy. Learning all he could about engines and how they worked from his blacksmith mentor Giorgio Ripamonti, young Carlo devoted every possible moment to his ideas for a motor cycle, although at this stage he had no idea of how he might manufacture or sell his dream. But when he did finally create his dream 'in the metal', Ripamonti was a great help in bringing the frame and cycle parts together.

By 1915 young Carlo had formulated a loose specification in his mind. His new machine would have a 500cc engine, built in unit with the gearbox and with the cylinder barrel in a horizontal position. This was partly to keep the centre of gravity low and create the lowest possible seating position, and largely to keep the engine running as cool as possible. But his dreams were to be shelved for three years as Italy went to war, and Carlo Guzzi put on the uniform of the Italian army.

By chance, Guzzi learned that the new Italian Air Corps needed competent mechanics. His motor cycle experience, combined with his general knowledge of the internal combustion engine, made him a natural choice for training as an aviation mechanic, Completing the course with ease, he was assigned to a squadron which numbered among its pilots two young men, Tenente Giovanni Ravelli and Tenente Giorgio Parodi, who were to influence Guzzi's life and make his dream come true. In between keeping their Ansaldo biplanes flying, the three men planned the creation of the ultimate Italian motor cycle. The loss of Giovanni Ravelli before the end of 1918 was a shattering blow to Guzzi and Parodi, but it strengthened their resolve to succeed.

At the time when Carlo Guzzi was creating his first motor cycle, the Italian magazine *Moto Cyclismo* was the leading organ of motor-cycling in the country and in December 1920 it announced the introduction of a new name in motor-cycling as Moto Guzzi in Mandello del Lario launched its new machine on to the market in the half-litre sector. The magazine described the GP prototype and then moved on to the new production model which was to be offered from the beginning of 1921. Carlo Guzzi and Giorgio Parodi had arrived – and so had their new motor cycles. They would never look back, quickly becoming Italy's premier motor cycle maker.

Tipo Normale (Standard Type or Model) was the name given to Moto Guzzi's first production model. It was in principle a simplified version of the prototype. Its frame was virtually identical to that of the prototype, and the 500cc engine had a bore and stroke of 88 x 82mm, slightly over square, but instead of the prototype's four valves, the Tipo Normale was fitted with only two, in a most unusual arrangement. The concept of having the inlet valve in an overhead position and the exhaust valve at the side (ioe = inlet over exhaust) was not an uncommon design concept, but to fit the exhaust valve overhead and use a side valve for the inlet certainly was unusual. This was the configuration of Carlo Guzzi's Normale engine design. He reasoned that the valve most in need of cooling (the exhaust) should be directly in the line of the airflow – and in a horizontal engine, with the cylinder head facing forward, the exhaust valve was the one directly in line with the airflow. Its overhead position allowed the exhaust porting to be more direct and made for better scavenging of gases. The valve was opened by a pushrod from the cam to a rocker shaft and closed by means of a hair spring, while the inlet valve was opened directly by the cam via a short tappet, and closed by means of an orthodox coil-spring. The cast-iron cylinder head was held in place by three long bolts fastening into the crankcase. The piston was made of aluminium alloy and had four compression rings in two pairs and two oil control rings. It was linked to the crankshaft by means of a tubular-section nickel steel connecting rod, running on oil-scrolled bronze bearings.

The one-piece crankshaft was also made of nickel steel and ran in large diameter bearings. It was mounted in a vertically split two-piece aluminium alloy crankcase with semi-automatic lubrication, a hand-operated pump sending oil from the main tank to a small sump under the crankcase, from which a gear-driven pump circulated it. There was no scavenge pump in the early engines, the oil system being total loss until a return pump was installed in the revised design during 1922. Fuel came via a British Amac carburettor, with sparks provided by a Bosch Type ZE shielded magneto.

Another pioneering Guzzi feature was the three-speed gearbox constructed in unit with the engine, a highly advanced concept for its time and one that was not widely adopted by other manufacturers until many years later. The sliding cog hand change unit was simple, solid and reliable, so furthering Moto Guzzi's early reputation for durable, value-for-money machines. The early models were also capable of hauling a sidecar around: not quickly, but reliably and reasonably economically. In fact Carlo Guzzi designed his own sidecar chassis around the Normale in 1925, with a four-point mounting and a very rugged frame design. The Normale continued in production only until late 1924, by which time the company's reputation had been firmly established.

A solid and reliable design, the Normale led to the introduction, in 1922, of a racing machine, the C2V (Corsa Duevalvole), with two pushrod overhead valves. The old EOI engine design had served its purpose and the manufacturing volumes of Moto Guzzi were now high enough to sustain the production of an improved and more powerful design, following more closely the original Guzzi e Parodi prototype. The C2V was the first of a long line of purpose-built racing Guzzis, but it was not the first racing Moto Guzzi of all! Carlo Guzzi had been approached by two well-known Italian racers, Mario Cavedini and Aldo Finzi. (Finzi was not only a sporting motor-cyclist, he was also a Member of Parliament.) They wanted motor cycles to enter the so-called 'North South Raid', an event which ran between Milan and Naples. The only two Moto Guzzis built at the time (actually one Moto Guzzi and the GP prototype) were accordingly entered for the race by Carlo Guzzi. Finzi finished in 22nd place, just behind Cavedini on the prototype. Moto Guzzi's racing career had begun, even though Carlo Guzzi had declared himself disinterested in racing.

The advanced design of Carlo Guzzi's GP prototype is clear to see, especially when compared with other machines of the day. The frame design is remarkably similar to many a frame of much more modern times. The four-valve engine was advanced but expensive, so in those early days it did not reach production. However, the unit gearbox did make it into production. The horizontal engine position was copied later by others, as it allowed both the centre of gravity and the rider's saddle position to be kept low.

The C2V was Moto Guzzi's first truly sporting model, the original example being built in 1923. The two-valve engine had parallel overhead valves and was again horizontally mounted in unit with the gearbox. The Corsa Duevalvole was a fine machine and was the first red Moto Guzzi. However, within a year, it was succeeded by the C4V, the Corsa Quattrovalvole and so the C2V reverted to the familiar olive green finish as it was offered for sale to the general public. This one, finished in green and carrying racing numbers, is how a private entrant's machine would have looked. It can be seen in the Mandello del Lario Museum.

The heart of the matter. The Quattrovalvole engine, of which 486 examples were built between 1924 and 1933, was the first Guzzi racing engine to carry the prefix 'C' in the number stamped on the casing. This particular engine is no. C29, a 1924 example. Three versions were produced in the unit's nine-year life: the original C4V, the 4VTT and the 4VSS. With its British carburettor and German magneto, it was a truly cosmopolitan product.

The C4V (Corsa Quattrovalvole – Racing Four-Valve) was introduced in 1924. The bevel-driven single overhead camshaft four-valve engine design signalled a return to the original concept of Carlo Guzzi's Guzzi e Parodi GP1. It was this very machine which brought Guido Mentasti the 1924 European Championship. It was the fastest 500cc motor cycle around for a while, having a top speed of just under 100mph. But despite its advanced engine, ultimately producing an amazing 32bhp, the unsprung frame and hand gear-change, with the old three-speed unit, saw the C4V fall from grace towards the end of its nine-year production life. Mentasti's works racer survives to this day in the Guzzi Museum.

Guido Mentasti, one of the leading riders of his time, was Europe's champion in 1924 and heart-throb of many a young lady follower of motor cycle sport. Mentasti would have signed this studio portrait on the glass negative (hence the signature appears in white on the print). Leather riding gear was now typical wear for all racing motor-cyclists and the scarf, white here but not for long on the track, was also typical, as it kept out dust and protected the rider's neck.

1924 the Corsa Quattrovalvole
(C4V) went into production in limited
numbers for sale to private entrants
who wanted to make their mark in
motor cycle racing. Pietro Ghersi was
the first man to put Moto Guzzi on the
racing map with the C4V, winning its
first event, the Circuito del Lario, at an
average speed of 67.630km/h. (This
may not seem very fast by today's
standards, but on the unmade roads of
the time it was a remarkable
achievement.) Guido Mentasti finished
second and another Guzzi was fourth in
that event. This triumph was soon
followed up with another magnificent
win at the Circuito di Cremona, where
the C4V also set a world record for the
flying Ten Kilometres at over 80mph.

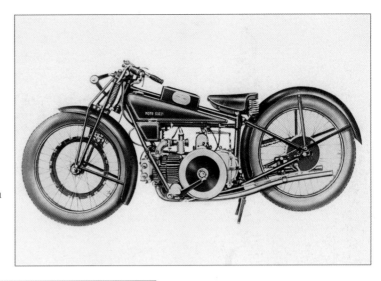

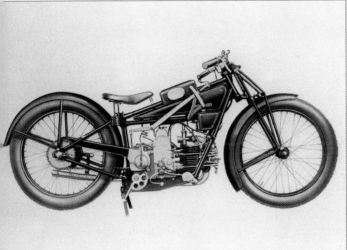

For 1925 the C2V (Corsa Duevalvole)
was also offered as a 'production'
racer. The two-valve engine was clearly
no adversary for its four-valve sibling,
but it brought racing within the
financial reach of a few more would-be
champions. The principal competition
in those days came from Britain, where
Norton, AJS, Sunbeam and Velocette
were leading the way, and from other
Italian manufacturers such as Bianchi
(for which Tazio Nuvolari was to ride
before he moved on to fame and
fortune with Alfa Romeo and Auto
Union) and Gilera, which many years
later the great Geoff Duke made a
household name.

Now provided with Italian
'sparks' by means of a
Magneti Marelli magneto,
the engine of the 1925
C2V model was a
masterpiece of engineering
'cleanliness', with the
engine in unit with the
gearbox and everything
tidily positioned and
attached to its
neighbouring component.
It was relatively easy to
install and remove, and the
whole assembly was lighter
than it would have been
had the gearbox been
separate from the engine.

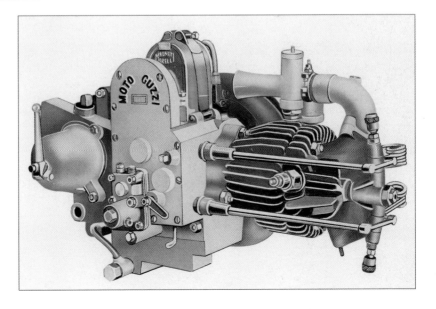

CHAPTER THREE

ESTABLISHING THE LINE

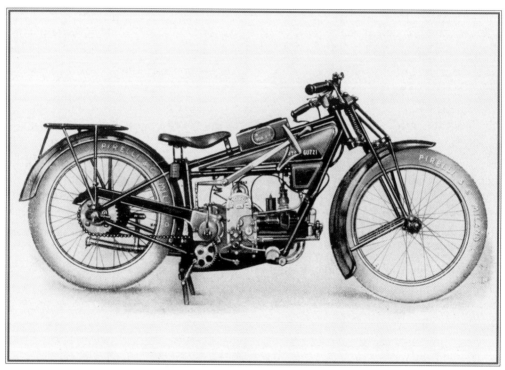

The 1925 Sport 500 was a roadgoing machine that looked very like the C2V. This was partly because it was built on the same frame. Beginning life in 1923, the Sport 500 was the successor to the Normale, using the same opposed valve engine design (exhaust-over-inlet) as the earlier model. The parcel grid over the rear wheel immediate showed that this was not a C2V, but no doubt many a 'cafe racer' of the 1920s would have been happy to remove the grid to improve the illusion.

By the end of 1923 Moto Guzzi had become a name to be reckoned with. The Normale had established the company's reputation for reliability in the field of production motor cycles, while the C2V had become the benchmark for competition machinery. But it was time to move on. The Normale needed a successor to keep abreast of market trends, and the racing scene needed a more advanced machine to keep its competitors at bay. As a consequence, the next model in the production line was to be the Sport, while Carlo Guzzi pulled out the drawings of his original GP for another look at the four-valve engine design.

The new production model, the Sport, combined the Normale engine and gearbox with the frame of the C2V racing model, so it could fairly be said that from the very beginning Moto Guzzi motor cycles benefited from the company's competition experience. The longer wheelbase of the C2V's duplex frame was brought together with the in-unit engine and gearbox in order to reduce slightly the weight of the new production machine. It also made the new model a little faster and endowed it with improved roadholding – enough to sell over four thousand examples in five years, which put the average production at sixteen machines a week – not bad for a company that grew from a very small workshop opposite Mandello del Lario's railway station.

While the Sport engine was based on the Normale power unit, it had a higher compression ratio (4.5:1 instead of 4:1) and improved engine speed. The engine could now rev to just under 4,000rpm and power was improved by around 50 per cent. Bore and stroke remained the same at 88 x 82mm, giving a displacement of 498.4cc, though with the higher running speed it could turn in 13bhp at 3,800rpm (compared with the original model's 8.5bhp at 3,400rpm). The British AMAC carburettor was still used, as was the three-speed hand change gearbox, transmitting the power from the engine to the chain-driven rear wheel.

Throughout the early development of Moto Guzzi motor cycles, ideas were focused on improving the ride and rear wheel handling. Carlo and Giuseppe Guzzi worked together on a new design, and finally, in 1928, the new GT model appeared. This was one of the first motor cycles to be equipped with rear wheel suspension. Its handling was not adversely affected by the softer and more comfortable rear end, and it was very popular in the market-place for its sheer comfort and handling stability. Within two years the GT became the GT16, now using the engine and basic frame of the Sport's successor, the Sport 15. The sprung frame of the early GT models, however, was not widely trusted – for no apparent reason – and fewer examples were sold than expected.

The Sport models, on the other hand, brought continuing success to Moto Guzzi. The Sport 14 succeeded the original model in 1929 and sold over 4,250 examples in under two years. This achievement was bettered by the next model in the line, the Sport 15. The most significant visual difference was the Sport 15's saddle tank, which gave it a much more modern appearance. Almost 6,000 Sport 15s were sold before the Model 'V' took its place and led the company into a new era. Two of the most successful features of the Moto Guzzi machines had been the low centre of gravity, which allowed a particularly stable ride, and the low position of the saddle, which made the motor cycle suitable for riders of almost any height. Carlo Guzzi himself was not a tall man and so appreciated the problems faced by the shorter rider on many contemporary machines.

Moto Guzzi's Model 'V' introduced a basic engine design that was to endure for more than thirty years through a series of models. It was still a 500cc unit, still with the bore and stroke of 88 x 82mm. The gearbox which accompanied this powerplant was also to last for some time, while the motor cycle into which they were installed brought a style of design which was to be identified with Mandello del Lario for over twenty years. Compare a 1934 'V' with a 1967 Falcone and you will see what I mean. However, the 'V', and its companions/successors, the GTV, GTW and GTC, were all more sporting machines than tourers. So Carlo Guzzi came up with the Model 'S', a more economical and robust machine able to sustain all the rigours expected of the touring motor cycle.

The 500cc Guzzi engine was also pressed into service as the power unit for a range of light commercial vehicles. In those days Italy had no oil reserves of its own, so even at the end of the 1920s fuel economy was important. Thus, in 1928, was born the first of Moto Guzzi's Motocarro models, starting a line that continued through to 1980. The Motocarro symbolised Italian light transport, with open-bodied trucks, delivery vans and even military vehicles based on the same chassis.

During 1926 a 250cc Moto Guzzi was developed, it being the company's intention to move downmarket with a view to increasing its market penetration. As well as meeting the demand for a lower-powered machine than the familiar 500, the 250 model would also be suitable for competition purposes. A 250 was duly entered for the 1926 Isle of Man Junior TT; although it didn't win, its participation marked the start of the line that would include the Albatros and the Gambalunghino, and established a winning tradition that would span three decades. Moto Guzzi was now an Italian tradition – the line was established.

e powerhouse of the Sport was the opposed valve Guzzi engine that had already established a reputation for ng virtually unburstable. You can see from this picture why Carlo Guzzi chose to adopt the unorthodox design a of placing the exhaust valve in the overhead position. With the engine lying horizontal and the cylinder ad facing the direction of travel, it was obvious to Guzzi that the right place for the hottest area of the engine s closest to the wind, hence exhaust-over-inlet.

e 500 Sport was a big chunky bike and was well able to take on a sidecar. Indeed, Moto Guzzi was offering this nbination in 1925 as an ex-works production vehicle, with full road equipment, including lamps. The sidecar was zzi-built and the motor cycle built to pull it was equipped with a front wheel brake operated from a lever on the ht handlebar. Note that the 500 Sport had no shock absorber to the forks, but they probably weren't considered essential, as riders, especially of sidecar combinations, wouldn't be going very fast on the roads of the time.

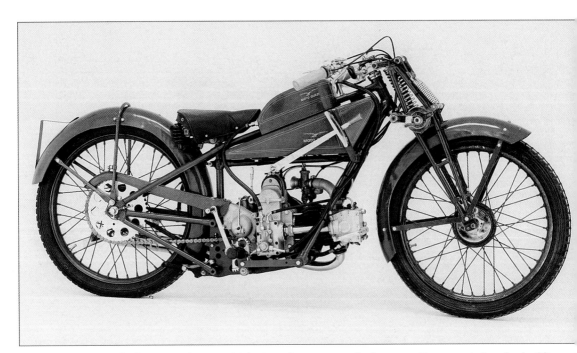

After five years in the business, during which time the company had won quite a reputation for building r[e]
race-winners,. Moto Guzzi decided it was time to build a machine for entry into what was then (and still
according to many racing enthusiasts) the world's leading motor cycle race, the Isle of Man Tourist Trophy. Ca[r]
Guzzi created a 250 machine, modelled largely on the Quattrovalvole 500, retaining the bevel drive to t[
overhead camshaft, but with only two valves. This little machine's first outing to the TT was in 1926, when [
outstanding performance by Pietro Ghersi brought the Guzzi 250 home into second place – only to be disqualif[
because the make of spark plug declared on the entry form was not the make in the engine at the finish of t[
race. Despite this setback, the Guzzi 250 was to be the master of its class for almost thirty years. By 1930 t[
250SS (below), purely a factory team machine, was equipped with a foot-changed three-speed gearbox. The f[
brake pedal had been moved from left to right and the machine was fitted with Brampton forks, probably the b[
type available for road racing at that time.

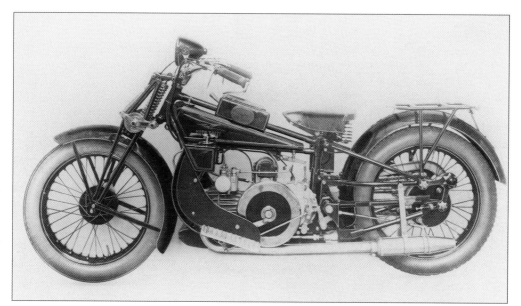

Carlo Guzzi recognised that one of the biggest shortfalls in terms of comfort on motor cycles was the lack of rear suspension. With the GT, announced in 1928, he solved that problem. A strong steel box sat longitudinally under the engine and contained four springs which reacted against a sliding member located in the rear end of the box and connected to the bottom link of the swinging arm. This Moto Guzzi GT was truly a Grand Tourer of considerable comfort and much improved handling, but it took a while to persuade the motor-cycling public to accept its reliability. Even so, between 1928 and 1934, when the original GT model was discontinued, only 754 examples were built. This is a 1929 model.

By 1929 the solid reliability of the Moto Guzzi 500 had been proven and, in addition to the sidecar version of the Sport, the decision was made to expand into a commercial application of this fine motor cycle. The result was the Veicolo di Transporto, forerunner of the highly successful Motocarro. A chain-driven tricycle, powered by the 500 Normale engine, it had a simple wooden body and was capable of carrying quite a load. This launched Moto Guzzi into a whole new field of profitable manufacture.

Soon after launching the Veicolo di Transporto Carlo Guzzi realised that his 500cc e-o-i engine had considerable potential for sale on its own, and the manufacture of engines without frames meant that greater profits could be made from the manufacturing facilities available with no further capital investment. Thus the Auxiliary Power Unit went into production to provide power for pumps, static generators and many other applications. It was sold in large numbers to the Italian armed forces and public services, such as fire brigades, too.

The Moto Guzzi Sport had developed into the Sport 14 by 1929, which in turn gave way to the Sport 15 in 1931. The saddle-tank brought Guzzi into the 'modern age', though features such as the hand gear-change and the original exhaust-over-inlet valve 500 engine were to remain in production for some time yet. This model stayed in production up to 1939 with few major changes and sold more than any other Guzzi model at the time. It was comfortable, reliable and relatively inexpensive for a 500cc machine. This picture shows the deluxe version, with chrome-plated fuel tank, wheel rims and fittings.

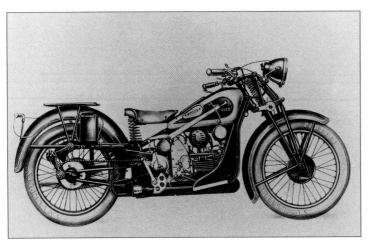

The GT Sport 15 also joined the model line-up in 1931, with leg shields for the touring motor-cyclist. The battery position had changed, being mounted higher on the GT version. Friction-type shock absorbers also appeared on the GT variant, allowing a more comfortable ride over 'grand touring' distances. In 1935 Dell'Orto carburettors replaced the Amals previously used.

CHAPTER FOUR

WIDENING THE RANGE AND WINNING RACES

Guzzi's first four-cylinder machine was built in 1930 as a racing prototype. It had many advanced features, including transverse mounting of the engine. It was supercharged with a Cozette blower and had dual ignition provided by a pair of Bosch magnetos. The engine and gearbox certainly filled the space available and this machine should have been far more successful than it proved to be. Hand gear-change didn't help its performance, but general unreliability proved the real handicap and so within quite a short time it was abandoned.

Having won the European Motor Cycle Championship in 1924 with the Sport 14, Moto Guzzi was now set to consolidate its position both on the track and in the market-place. The Sport 14 had put the company on the map as a serious manufacturer of sound, reliable racing motor cycles, while the 250 had led to the introduction of a range of smaller Moto Guzzis to supply a market not previously available to the company. And of course, there were the new commercial motor tricycles in the form of the Motocarro range. In a constant quest for improvement, Moto Guzzi's experimental department always had something new in its workshop. In 1930 a four-cylinder supercharged engine was laid transversely across the frame of a racing motor cycle, rather in the fashion of motor cycles of sixty years or so later. The Quattro Cilindri looked more fearsome than it proved to be on the track, but it was a useful development exercise and out of it, a little over a year later, came many of the ideas for the three-cylinder (Tre Cilindri) touring model, which also had its engine mounted transversely. Introduced in 1932, this three-cylinder machine was perhaps too advanced for its time, as only a few pre-production examples were built and sold before the idea was abandoned. Only one example is known to have survived and it is now in the Moto Guzzi museum collection at Mandello del Lario.

With its huge potential for young rider sales, the lightweight end of the market was to be Moto Guzzi's next focus of attention and two new models, the P175 and P250, would trail-blaze the new direction for the company. That's not to say that they abandoned the old faithful 500 single, but the arrival of the 250 led in turn to the creation of the first Guzzi V-Twin: the 500 Bicilindrica, with an unsprung frame, was to enjoy an almost invincible racing career for almost twenty years. The most significant event of that career was Stanley Woods' magnificent Senior TT win in 1935.

Selling motor cycles for profit was still Carlo Guzzi's main aim, however, so the continuing development and growth of a range of machinery for all sectors of the Guzzi market was all-important. The Motocarro was a 500 horizontal single-powered lightweight truck which preceded the American motor tricycles made famous in the 1930s. It was offered initially as a commercial product, but was soon offered to the Italian armed forces, too. The GT, a 500 single motor cycle, was another model that became recognised as a military machine, and it led in turn to the Alce and Trialce machines which variously carried people and armament to further Mussolini's military causes at home and overseas. Support for Mussolini was secondary, though, to Guzzi and Parodi, as their principal objective remained the winning of lucrative government contracts for military and police machinery, as these supported the company through an otherwise precarious business era.

It may not have been Carlo Guzzi's personal aim, but within the company there was certainly great determination to build a motor cycle able to win the Isle of Man Tourist Trophy Race. It took two years from the public launch of the Bicilindrica to achieve that goal, but achieve it the Mandello firm certainly did. A rigorous development programme was undertaken, and a suitable rider was found in the form of the great Irishman Stanley Woods. He had already made a name for himself with Cotton and Norton, winning six TTs already, and would later go on to even greater fame with that other British industry leader, Velocette. But for the present, his target was victory in the TT in 1935. Umberto Todero tells of the close friendship that grew up between him and Stanley, and the very close liaison they shared in the development of the race winner. Nothing was left to chance and every feature that Stanley Woods criticised was modified until he was completely happy and at one with the machine he was to ride.

Before winning the 500TT in 1935, Stanley Woods had also entered, and won, the Junior event on a Guzzi 250, hotly pursued by his team-mate, the popular local rider Omobono Tenni. Having already put up some sparkling performances for Moto Guzzi, Tenni had chased home his team-mate in the Junior TT. Tenni was to become Italy's most popular national rider and his close association with both Woods and Todero enhanced his fine reputation. After the triumphs of 1935, Stanley Woods moved on to Velocette, while the name Moto Guzzi was on the lips of every TT fan. This was the first time that the company had achieved such success on a 'foreign' field – but it wouldn't be the last.

As a result of winning the government contracts, Moto Guzzi were able to engage in a great deal of engineering development. They didn't just win military contracts, either, as a range of police forces in Italy selected Moto Guzzis for both two-wheeled patrols and escort duties from the early 1930s onwards. It is known that Benito Mussolini regarded Moto Guzzi in a favourable light, as he did Alfa Romeo, the car maker located some 50km to the south in Milan. There is a fine picture of Mussolini (*see* p. 6) standing in the back of his Alfa Romeo Ministeriale car, flanked by a pair of Moto Guzzi-mounted police escorts, as he passed through Reggio Calabria during a pre-war rally. In this position of relative favour, Moto Guzzi engineers were able to quietly pursue development work ready for a return to peacetime production – when it came.

The Quattro Cilindri engine. Note the vertical cooling fins on the cylinder barrels – far more efficient conductors of airflow on a horizontally mounted engine. The magnetos were tucked in just ahead of the blower, which was neatly mounted on top of the gearbox. It was a superb piece of engineering.

By 1932 Carlo Guzzi had decided to move into the lightweight motor cycle market, a sector which had be neglected, even ignored, by the other major manufacturers in Italy. Vehicle taxation in the country favour smaller machines and Guzzi seized the opportunity to increase sales by updating a few design ideas. Thus w born the 'P' Series, beginning with the P175, which was soon to be followed by the P250 model, illustrated her

Announced at around the same time as the low tax 'P' Series was Moto Guzzi's 500cc Tre Cilindri (Three-Cylinder) grand tourer. Aimed at the long-haul rider, the Tre Cilindri used the multi-cylinder concept with the object of smoothing out engine vibration while providing sufficient power and torque to give a thoroughly comfortable ride. Coupled to a three-speed gearbox, the machine could have been a very popular model, but its design was rather too far ahead of its time and so only a few were built. Only one survives, in the museum at Mandello del Lario.

The engine of the Tre Cilindri shows typical Guzzi characteristics, although the flywheel was now enclosed. Fuel passed through a single British Amal carburettor, down a long induction tract to the three cylinders; this rather odd design still enabled the engine to deliver 25bhp and pull the machine along at over 80mph.

Commercial vehicles were of growing importance to the economic growth of Moto Guzzi in the 1930s. The sheer durability of the Guzzi frame and the opposed valve 500cc engine almost guaranteed sales, as there was very little competition available in the market-place. The Moto Triclico Model 32 of 1932 paved the way for significant expansion of production of the outstanding workhorse that was to become the Motocarro. Many of these vehicles were built for military applications up to and during the Second World War.

By 1933/4 the racing 250 had been thoroughly modernised and for the 1934 racing season featured a foot change gearbox. English Brampton forks carried the front wheel and provided far better roadholding than anything else available for road racing. Note the plug spanner adjacent to the rear wheel, which allowed the rider who experienced fouled spark plugs to make a change on the road. The only condition attached to plug change was that the rider had to use the same make and type as was fitted to his machine at the start of the race.

ch was the sheer ruggedness of
oto Guzzi motor cycles, especially
e GT Series, that in 1933 the
lian government, when
panding its military budget,
ught the Guzzi GT17. Armed
otor cycles in those days were a
mmon item in military
ventories. This one is fitted with a
ght machine-gun, but it must have
en pretty cumbersome to ride
th the gun in place. The rider
rtainly could not have used the
eapon while in motion, especially
hen trying to change gear with his
ght hand!

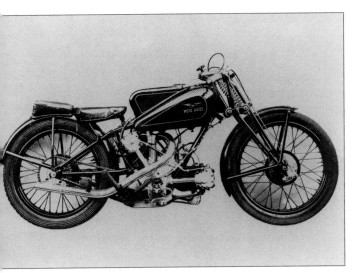

Apart from military and commercial
developments at Mandello del Lario,
there was another machine that set
Moto Guzzi apart from all its
competitors in the use of a twin-
cylinder engine. Basically the
Bicilindrica 500 consisted of two 250
cylinder barrels positioned at 120
degrees on a common crankcase. This
machine was to form the basis of
Mandello del Lario's racing successes
for almost twenty years, it's first
international milestone being Stanley
Woods' Senior TT Victory in 1935.
This is the original rigid frame version
of 1933.

eveloping the quarter-litre machine
stage further brought the PE250 to
e market in 1934. Still not really a
50, the PE had a sprung frame to
prove its saleability and proved to
e a thoroughly reliable machine. It
ld almost 1,600 examples before it
as superseded in 1939 by the true
50cc Airone.

Guzzi big singles still represented the mainstream of the company's product range and the Models V and GT were the mainstays of that line. The rigid-framed V (above) was in production between 1934 and 1940, using the old three-speed gearbox to keep costs down. The 'GTV' (below) was a long-distance tourer, with sprung frame, footshields and four-speed gearbox, which remained in production, with modifications, until the appearance of the Falcone in 1948.

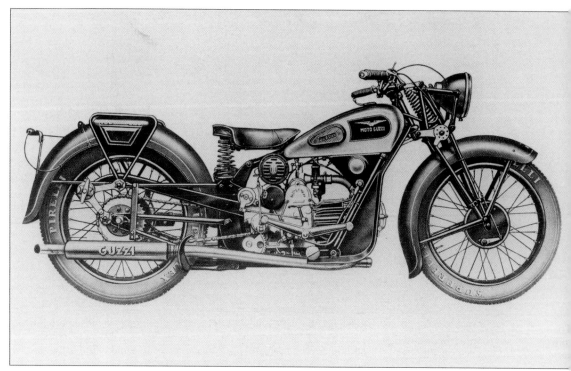

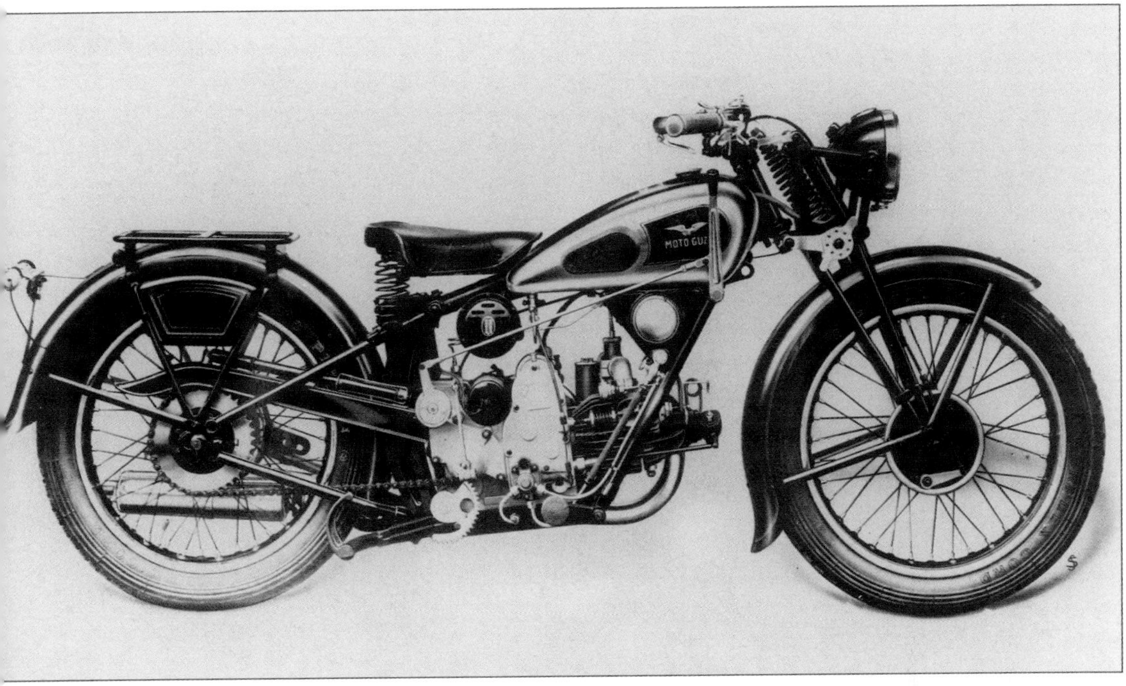

he dual overhead valve V-type engine did not completely replace the original opposed valve (e-o-i) design, for ;uzzi perceived a gap in the market-place for a low cost 500. This gap was filled by the Type 'S', aimed at the onservative-thinking Moto Guzzi user who wanted a low cost commuting 500. Like the V model, this machine ad a rigid frame and had an optional preselect hand-change. The GTS version had the same engine, legshields nd a four-speed gearbox, combined with the sprung frame of the GTV. Over 6,500 of the two variants were built efore they were discontinued in 1940.

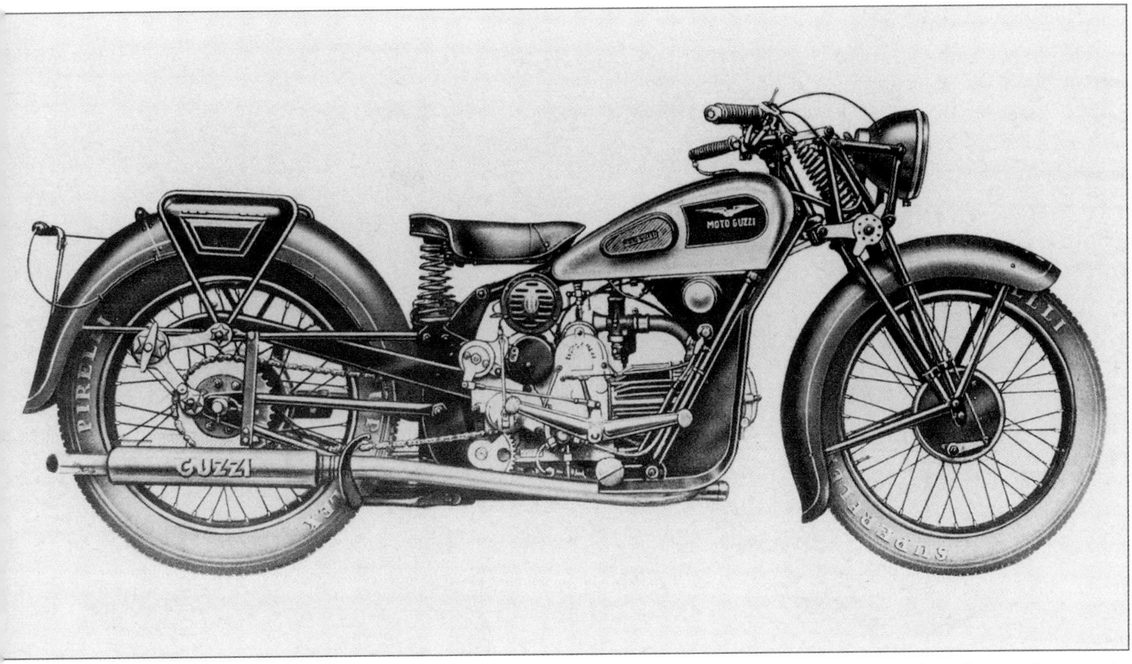

The GTV of 1935 was a 'cleaned-up' version of the earlier model and was a thoroughly handsome big single ourer. It was regarded by many people as an ideal sidecar machine and many Guzzi GTVs were pressed into service in that way, as substitutes for small family cars. While many working Italians could afford a motor cycle and sidecar, the prices of cars of the day put them out of reach.

Racing was very important to Moto Guzzi and in 1935 the company finally achieved its ultimate goal – victory at the Isle of Man. The first victory came in the Junior TT, in which Irishman Stanley Woods secured a magnificent win. The 250TT Corsa was further proof of Guzzi's superiority in the quarter-litre class, though that TT win was also proof of Stanley's great skill.

Partnering Stanley Woods at the 1935 Junior TT was Omobono Tenni, one of Italy's rising stars of the day. Tenni was to prove himself one of the world's all-time greats, though in the 1935 TT he crashed and so did not feature in the results. Tenni was described by people at Mandello del Lario as one of the bravest and most calculating motor-cyclists ever to race for them.

his is the magnificent 'lean machine' ridden by Stanley Woods in the 1935 Senior TT. Woods was already a six
mes TT winner on Cotton and Norton machines, but this was his first on a Guzzi; it was also the first time that a
on-British machine had won the great international classic. It was an exciting machine and beat all the big
ngles.

Coming round Governor's Bridge to the finish, here's Stanley Woods winning by just four seconds
ahead of Scotsman Jimmy Guthrie's Norton. On the sixth lap Guthrie was in the lead and expected
to win, but Woods pulled out all the stops and pushed the Guzzi to over 125mph on the straights
to overhaul the leader and snatch victory.

For 1937 the GTC (Gran Turismo, Corsa) was produced to meet the demand for a 'production racer' in the Sport racing category, established that year. It was a street-legal machine with a 17-litre fuel tank, a 26bhp engine (the GTV produced only 18bhp), a sprung frame and a most odd-looking exhaust with four silencers (two each side). The higher engine power enabled the GTC to reach just under 100mph, though the roadholding and braking were strictly of GTV standard. In all, 161 examples were built up to 1939.

This is the robust GTV of 1937. Dual exhausts were a feature of this model, though they were of more modest design than those of the GTC. Note the rider-adjustable rear shock absorbers, a legacy from the sprung frame racing machines of the time. This model, along with the less expensive S Type, was the mainstay of Moto Guzzi production two-wheelers up to the Second World War and returned to production briefly after the war.

CHAPTER FIVE

CONTINUING DEVELOPMENT AND THE CLOUDS OF WAR

By 1937 the PES had evolved from the original P Series. This was a sporty model, still using the original three-speed gearbox, but of lighter weight than the standard PE and giving a performance of 72mph. This may not seem like much now, but in the late 1930s it was a fair turn of speed for a mildly modified quarter-litre production machine. Only seventy-five PES models were built for sale and a number of them were raced in clubman class events with modest success.

The P175 and P250 mentioned briefly in the last chapter merit closer attention here because these two smaller machines accounted for much of the development of Moto Guzzi's manufacturing strategy. The P175 was the first of the two but interest in the sub-200 motor cycle waned when certain concessions concerning machines with small engines (less than 200cc) were abolished. So the P250 was introduced, a P175 stretched to 232cc. The PL followed, with a 246cc engine, and that model grew into the PLS (the Egretta), and the PE followed that in 1939. The PE was better known as the Airone (Heron) and became a very popular model.

Also during 1939, a new model appeared for amateur racers. This was the 250cc Albatros. Produced specifically for use in races for non-professional entrants riding production machines, it was basically a works racing machine with no supercharger but with roadgoing fittings and electrics. It must have been the fastest street legal machine on the market in its day. Bird names had become the fashion with Moto Guzzi by now and the 500cc single-cylinder amateur race machine was named Condor.

Apart from its qualities as a machine, the Albatros had a particular significance for Moto Guzzi for this magnificent motor cycle heralded the career of an engineer who was to take the company to new heights of success. His name was Giulio Cesare Carcano and his first product, despite its price exceeding that of a Motocarro commercial motor tricycle, was a huge success, sweeping the board of amateur Italian motor cycle racing. Its engine differed from those of its predecessors, in that it had a single-piece crankshaft, pressure lubrication to the valve gear and truly 'square' bore/stroke dimensions of 68 x 68mm, giving a displacement of 246.8cc. Finished in bright red, with the Moto Guzzi logo placed on amaranth panels on the fuel-tank sides, it was a truly handsome and thoroughly successful machine.

But the clouds of war were looming large as 1939 advanced, and as Hitler's armies advanced into Poland it became clear that before long the whole of Europe would become involved in this new world conflict. Benito Mussolini did not like the British or their empire, especially as it affected what he saw as 'his' Africa so, although many Italians had closer affinities with the British than with the Germans of the day, Il Duce threw in his lot with Hitler's Axis Powers. When war did come, there were some very mixed emotions in Italy. Until June 1940 many Italian-engineered products used British accessories or were manufactured under licence from Britain. Moto Guzzi, for example, used British electrical components, carburettors and tyres, while down the road in Milan Alfa Romeo had been manufacturing British-designed aero engines under licence for years. All that was to change.

Italy went to war in the summer of 1940. The Italian forces had already proved their capabilities in the Spanish Civil War, with the Legionara Aviazione in particular winning respect for their skills and professionalism. Their first major campaign of the Second World War took place in the North African desert, but it proved to be a rather different story. The Italian troops seemed to have little enthusiasm for Hitler's war and they walked away in their thousands. But their equipment was beyond reproach. The aircraft, trucks, cars and motor cycles all performed as they were asked to do, with a few exceptions. The Moto Guzzis they operated were built for a wide range of activities. There were solo machines with one or two seats, solo machines with machine-guns, and motor cycle and sidecar combinations with either passenger seats, gun platforms or cargo-carriers. There were also passenger-carrying Motocarro tricycles, anti-aircraft gun-carriers, light field gun carriers and load carriers.

As the war progressed, these machines were subjected to some of the most gruelling operating conditions conceivable, from the rough dusty terrain of the Western Desert, back across Sicily and up the Italian peninsula in all weathers, through mud and across unmade tracks and open country. Some inevitably broke down, but in the main these machines proved the durability and sheer gutsiness of Moto Guzzi's products. They were also used by the British forces in North Africa and by the Allies as they advanced up the Italian mainland. As the Germans came down into Northern Italy during 1943, they too found Moto Guzzi motor cycles and Motocarros at least the equal of their own BMWs and Zundapps – and Moto Guzzis were made available to them.

The GT17 was the first of Moto Guzzi's military/police motor cycles and its roots lay in the Sport 15, with an exhaust-over-inlet valve 500cc engine and three-speed hand-change gearbox. It was supplied to the armed forces in green and sand, and a number were also supplied to the Milizia della Strada (Traffic Police). A four-speed gearbox and a few minor chassis modifications updated it to the GT20 in 1939. The GT17 had proved itself in the Abyssinian War of 1935–6 and the 4,800-odd built served their masters well through the major conflict which followed (there were even examples in use on the Russian front). The GT20 was an interim model, for the most famous of all military Guzzis was the Alce (Elk), which began to be delivered in 1939. Almost 6,500 were produced, nearly 700 of which were sidecar-equipped, by the end of 1945. The Alce retained the EOI engine and four-speed gearbox.

Production of the Trialce three-wheeler was much less, with just over 1,700 examples manufactured. These were used in all the same theatres of war as the GT17 and the Alce. In adverse conditions, the Trialce offered better stability than the two-wheelers for load-carrying and was better able to cross rough terrain. All in all, Moto Guzzi made a substantial contribution to the nation's war effort, with over 13,000 thousand machines seeing service. Guzzis continue to serve the nation to this day, in military and police versions.

Aimed at proving the worth of the PES, Moto Guzzi prepared one for entry in the 1937 Milano–Taranto roa race. It didn't win, but it did finish and achieved its goal in proving that the PES was a capable and reliable litt motor cycle. This particular PES achieved just over 78mph on the road and enhanced the reputation of th ordinary production P Series.

Aiming at producing a low cost 500 utility motor cycle, Moto Guzzi introduced the Model L in 1938. Using th rigid frame of the Model S, together with the opposed valve engine of the S, this new economy model had number of cost-cutting features which distinguished it from its siblings. For example, and most obviously, th forks were no longer of the girder type, but were of pressed steel in the same general shape. Also made of presse steel was the rear combined luggage carrier and toolbox. But by this time much of Moto Guzzi's time was devote to the manufacture of military vehicles, two- and three-wheeled.

uring the same year that the Model L was launched, production of the Model ER Motocarro began in earnest. his is clearly a civilian example, since it has a plated fuel tank, but the basis of the chassis was the same hatever the application the Motocarro was put to. You can see here the interesting combination of tubular otor cycle frame and light truck box-section chassis. Some 5,143 examples were built between 1938 and 1942.

his view of a complete ER shows a fairly heavy truck body subframe, especially the part supporting the rear uspension. It had to be pretty robust as many of the tracks and road surfaces on which the machines would perate were quite testing for any vehicle's suspension and structure. The bodies were mostly made of timber, aturing fixed sides and headboard but a hinged tailgate. Some even had hydraulic tipping rams to adapt them as nall dump-trucks.

Racing was still an important issue at Mandello del Lario, even in 1938, and while the production lines concentrated on machines that would make money for Moto Guzzi, the race shop was concentrating on its next model, the 250cc supercharged single. Despite a very compact power unit, the power package was a very tight fit in the frame. This machine was better suited to short-distance record-breaking than racing.

The powerpack of the Supercharged 250, nicknamed 'Gerolamo' (after the hunchback of Notre Dame) because of the Guzzi-built Cozette blower positioned above the gearbox. Note also the enormous expansion chamber above the cylinder barrel. This 246cc engine ran up to 7800rpm, at which speed it delivered a remarkable 38bhp. Unfortunately the engine lacked long-distance endurance capability and so its racing career was a somewhat chequered affair. In alcohol-fuelled form, the engine produced an even more remarkable 48bhp and took numerous speed records, some of the most remarkable being with sidecars at speeds up to 138.26mph.

his is the second version of the Supercharged 250, built and tuned specifically for Omobono Tenni to attack a ries of 250cc endurance records in December 1938. The enlarged fuel tank is obvious, and behind it sits the oil nk. The huge expansion chamber attached to the engine in the preceding picture has been replaced on this achine with a small chamber. Even so, it took records at speeds of well over 110mph.

s well as the blown 250, there was also the Albatros production 250cc racer, a development of the same assis. A young engineer named Giulio Cesare Carcano was recruited to assist Carlo Guzzi in the development of is new production racer. Carcano remained with Guzzi for many years and became the major influence in Guzzi cing design. The Albatros was strictly a production racing motor cycle, manufactured specifically for amateur cing riders. It was essentially the supercharged 250 without its blower and fitted with road equipment, and it as to reign supreme until 1949.

The Albatros in action in more modern times. Here's a 1939 example being ridden by Dutchman Bert Sonnebor at a Vintage Motor Cycle Club race meeting at Lydden in England during the 1990s. Beautifully restored, th machine is a fine example of Moto Guzzi's most successful 250 racer. It's adversaries today, as in the 1930 include makes such as Benelli, DKW, Excelsior and Rudge.

You could almost say this was an Albatros with a 500cc engine, for the Condor was indeed basically the sam design by Carlo Guzzi and Giulio Carcano. Equipped with the pushrod 500 engine, the Condor was aimed at th same market sector as the Albatros – the private entrant. The machine illustrated here finished second in its clas in the Milano–Taranto Corridori race. Road equipped, it was a handsome machine.

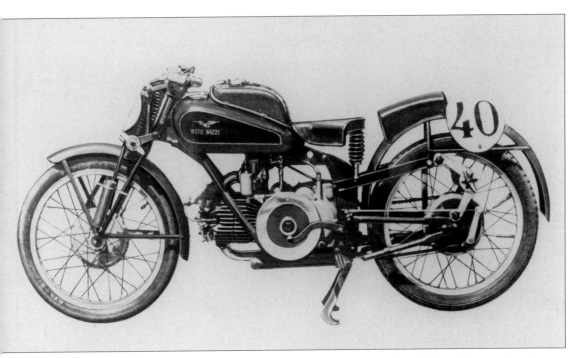

Ugo Prini took a class win in the Circuito del Lario of 1938 astride this Condor (although it was then known simply as a Model Nuova C). The Condor name was attached to the machine only after it had been offered in the market as the GTCL, in succession to the GTC. Interestingly, these two models, the 250cc Albatros and the 500cc Condor, were named respectively after the largest marine bird and the largest land bird in the world.

Italy's less ambitious and more realistic answer to Germany's 'People's Car' – the Volkswagen – was the 'People's Motor Cycle', which actually made it into production, although in somewhat limited numbers. Moto Guzzi's PL Ardetta was the least expensive model in the range at 3,950 Lire (or on government-sponsored terms at 170 Lire per month). The engine was now of 246cc displacement and was coupled to a three-speed hand- or foot-change gearbox. The Ardetta was painted grey with white lining, and 599 units were sold.

The Airone (Heron) was built around a pressed steel frame and was intended as the successor to the P Series motor cycles. It was originally labelled as a P model, but clearly the range needed a new name, so Airone it became. It was to become Italy's most popular lightweight motor cycle for fifteen years, being updated and modified until it could no longer compete with many machines of smaller engine size. It was finally pensioned off in 1957.

Italy's first military motor cycle of the Second World War was the military GTS, literally a militarised variant of the civilian GTS. The GTS was originally the 'sporty' version of the S and so the improved performance was a boon to its military users. But it wasn't designed specifically as a military machine, so it lacked many of the fittings expected of a typical service model.

The GT20 Model VT took the Milizia della Strada (the Highway Patrols) up a step from the Model S that they had been using for some time. The engine in this new creation was a developed version of the S type's unit and its aim was to give much better performance to the patrol motor cycle. Interestingly, it carried the dual silencer boxes of the earlier GTC. An odd-looking machine, the GT20 performed its task well and ran in service for several years, even though it was only produced as an interim machine, pending the arrival of the Alce.

The first Moto Guzzi to carry its model name on the tank was the Alce (Elk), perhaps because it was a military machine. The lack of additional fittings indicates that this example is a Monoposto model, a dispatch rider's machine. It was very similar in looks to the GT20, but certain detail features were different. Over 6,500 Alces, SuperAlces and Trialces were built.

Here is the Alce V Biposto (two-seater). 'So what's special about a pillion seat?' you may ask. Well, take a look at this for a two-seat motor cycle. The rear seat passenger sits well above the level of the rider because of the essential gap between his seat and the rear wheel. So the handlebars for the passenger also appear very high, but in actual fact, they're not as far above the seat as the rider's. This machine is relatively uncluttered, but has a heavier duty rear carrier framework to support ammunition boxes and similar loads. The engine on the V was the dual overhead valve 500, the armed forces at last seeing that the old opposed valve design was a bit dated and getting rather short on power.

Even in 1940, just before Benito Mussolini threw in his lot with Germany to form the Axis powers of the Second World War, Moto Guzzi was keen to race. This is the next stage of development of the supercharged 250 machine. By this time fuel injection was being investigated at Mandello del Lario; as well as various mechanical designs produced by the Guzzi team, a Fuscaldi-Caproni electromagnetic installation was also tried. But the demands of war deterred further development for a while.

The most amazing creation of 1940 was, without doubt, this three-cylinder racer. It was a most advanced design, using the engine as a stressed member of the frame. Another supercharged creation, this dual overhead camshaft power unit delivered an amazing 65bhp at 8000rpm out of 500cc – a power output equal to that of many a respectable 500cc sports racing car. With a top road speed of over 140mph, this bike could have been a world beater – but once again war intervened.

By 1940 the GTS was not only capable of carrying a light machine-gun, but Moto Guzzi had developed it into a firing platform as well. With an armoured front panel, which doubled as a wind deflector in the riding position, the machine was capable of being ridden in reasonable safety, while once the saddle was hinged back, the rider was able to adopt a lower position which enabled him to fire the weapon and be reasonably protected.

This is the Alce V, showing all the bracketry to carry a heavy machine-gun on one side and its supporting tripod on the other, with ammunition boxes as panniers. In addition, there is bracketry on the luggage carrier to support a radio transmitter/receiver. Note the high ground clearance of this model, which made it an ideal machine for use in the Western Desert campaign. When Alces fell into Allied hands after the fall of Libya, they were very much appreciated as solid reliable machines.

Also in 1940 the Alce V was adapted to sidecar operation and was named the Motocarrozzetta. A spare wheel was mounted on the back of the sidecar and a more than ample windscreen was fitted at the front. Other, more practical, sidecars were also fitted to the Alce, which saw service in this form in Greece, North Africa and the European war. On the home front, of course, the Motocarrozzetta was used by Italian forces under Mussolini, and against them by Italians, Americans and Britons. All spoke highly of the machine.

Another variation on the theme was the Trialce, seen here in high ground clearance load-carrier form as a chassis. The Trialce was essentially a military Motocarro which used the Alce front end. It was capable of hauling a payload of 800kg. They were used as load carriers, personnel carriers, gun carrier/platforms and ambulances in high chassis form.

At the other end of the Trialce scale was this staff vehicle. The Germans used cars for most officer transport, except for junior officers who mostly travelled in the sidecars of motor cycles. However, the Italians were more pragmatic about transport, and only senior Italian officers were afforded the luxury of transport by staff car – others travelled in the rear of Moto Guzzi Trialces.

The passenger-carrying version of the Trialce was available with a gun-mounting to accommodate a heavy machine-gun of the kind illustrated here. One might reasonably suppose that the gun was primarily intended for defence, though the calibre of the weapon shown could make it capable of taking on a company of infantry. These vehicles were used for forward scouting, so such an armament did have a purpose, especially for protection from ambush.

For sheer fire-power, though, try this. It's a truck-bodied Trialce with a full swivel-mounted 20mm cannon for anti-aircraft use. The Italian forces in the North African desert had been caught out more than once by low-flying enemy aircraft, so this kind of weapon would have been very useful, and was certainly capable of doing some pretty severe damage to approaching attackers from the air.

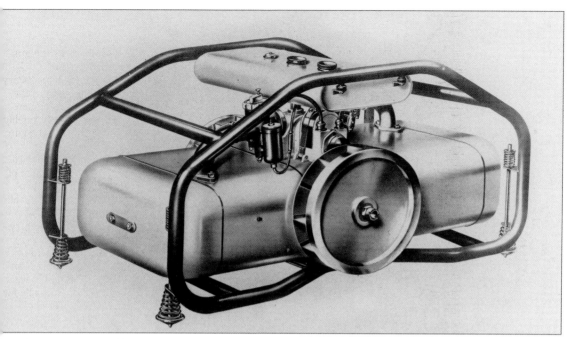

In 1942 Moto Guzzi produced a portable generator set powered by the FA flat-twin engine. It was developed for military use in the field and for emergency use in urban areas where main power supplies were severed through war damage. It looked a purposeful piece of equipment and certainly would have found widespread use in northern Italy during late 1943 and 1944, when the Americans were bombing northern towns.

This is the Model U engine of 1943, which powered later versions of the Alce and Trialce. It was now clear that the old opposed valve engine had had its day. After all, while the exhaust-over-inlet design made for a more efficient engine than dual side valves, most motor cycle engines were now dual overhead valve types and so an opposed valve unit could no longer produce the power essential for the kind of performance that riders wanted.

By 1944, with the end of the war in sight, Italian industry was beginning to look forward with a degree optimism, hoping that the conflict would soon be over and that peaceable Italians could get on with their live This machine is a pedal bicycle with a Moto Guzzi 30cc power unit which drove the cycle by means of a knurle wheel rotating in contact with the rear tyre of the bike.

Also in 1944 a newly designed utility 125cc motor cycle was built at Mandello del Lario, the object being provide low cost commuter transport for the workers who would rebuild postwar Italian industry. It was r typical of past Moto Guzzis, though it did have overhead valves and that characteristic 'bacon slicer' flywheel. T frame of this experimental model was a combination of steel tube and pressed steel fabrications. The forks we also of pressed steel.

CHAPTER SIX

NEW TIMES, NEW PRODUCTION

As 1945 brought the official end of the war (25 April was Liberation Day for Italy), so a civilianised GTV appeared, complete with sprung frame, for sale to the enthusiastic motor cyclist eager for a new machine after such a long wait. This GTV was very similar to the prewar model, but was easy to produce at Mandello del Lario, as the production tooling was still in use. The mudguards were slightly modified, being made more full for better weather protection, but otherwise this motor cycle looked very much like its prewar sibling.

As it became clear that the Italian people had endured enough of the deprivations and destruction of Adolf Hitler's war, the majority of the nation's armed forces laid down their arms in late 1943 and aligned themselves with the Anglo-American Alliance. They were under the provisional political leadership of Marshal Pietro Badoglio, who had been Mussolini's Chief of General Staff until he spoke out about Italy's disastrous invasion of Greece. The German response to Badoglio's administration was to move into northern and central Italy and establish Mussolini in the puppet government of what was called the Salo Republic (so-named because of the small northern town where it was located). Mussolini himself was housed 'for his own protection' in a villa on the shore of Lake Garda and was isolated from his 'government' by a heavily armed German guard.

Soon after Pietro Badoglio had changed sides, British-built aircraft began wearing the Italian red, white and green roundels. But the north of Italy was not so fortunate. Now under German occupation, things would get worse before they got better: raw materials would become harder to find and the process of manufacture would become somewhat precarious as restrictions tightened. Moto Guzzi continued to survive by producing motor cycles for their temporary new masters. Eventually, the inexorable advance of the Allied forces, combined with the weakening German hold on northern Italy, forced Hitler's troops out of Italy altogether, and the country was liberated on 25 April 1945. Mussolini was already dead and the new Italian Republic would soon be born.

In those difficult post-war days manufacturing companies had to be flexible to survive, turning their hands to almost anything. Moto Guzzi did not abandon its heritage and still made motor cycles, though the new machines were of a very different calibre from the pre-war models. For a while, racing would be no more than a dream, as the company's economic survival was all-important in an environment where governments were changing every few weeks for a time. The company's first post-war product idea was the Colibri ('humming bird'), a cycle-motor engine for installation on to ordinary pedal cycles, but this didn't reach production. It was followed by the first 'real' motor cycle, the 65cc Motoleggera ('leggera' = 'lightweight'). Launched in the spring of 1946, the Motoleggera proved to be so popular that over 50,000 had been sold by 1949, despite the difficulties in obtaining materials. The Motoleggera achieved the highest volume of production for a single motor cycle model manufactured in Italy up to that time.

As the process of peace and recovery advanced, the supply of raw materials became less fraught with problems and Moto Guzzi brought back into production the 250cc Airone and the GTV 500 to fill the needs of their traditional markets. It wasn't long before the GTV was succeeded by the GTW, which led to the Falcone via the Astore. On the racing front, the company revived the Albatros, and in 1946 introduced the 500cc Dondolino. This new racer was built in small numbers for sale to private entrants and won many races, major and minor, including the Milano–Taranto road event. It was during this same period that the Gambalunga – one of the most famous racing Guzzis – was produced. Another 500cc machine, it was manufactured between 1946 and 1951. A 250cc version of the same machine appeared in 1949 as the Gambalunghino.

The year 1950 brought one of the most interesting Moto Guzzi models yet – the Galletto. Another lightweight, everyday two-wheeler, it was to prove one of the most successful of its kind. Designed by Carlo Guzzi himself, it was basically a motor scooter with many of the characteristics of a conventional motor cycle. It had larger wheels than most scooters and so enjoyed the stability, and many of the handling features, of a larger machine. The Galletto started life as a 160cc machine but had grown to 192cc by the time it went out of production sixteen years later. It had many novel features, the most noticeable of which was probably the position of the spare wheel, lodged between the front wheel and the protective front valance.

By 1954 the now modified and improved Motoleggera was reborn as the Cardellino. Still a 65cc machine, it looked more like a 'real' motor cycle, with a larger tank, rear suspension with shock absorbers and telescopic front forks. Growing to 73cc in 1956, the Cardellino continued to be offered, with various modifications, until 1965. The engine was enlarged in 1962 to 83cc to make the machine more attractive to young riders, but with the disappearance of the legislation allowing lightweights to be run without registration plates, the popularity of this and similar models from other manufacturers dwindled. So when Moto Guzzi was reorganised in 1965, the Cardellino was dropped from the range.

By the end of the 1940s, Moto Guzzi was firmly established as the manufacturer of a range of high-quality motor cycles which had proven themselves in such gruelling events as the International Tourist Trophy Race. Gambalunghinos finished first and second in the 1947 Lightweight TT, though Freddie Frith's race ended in disaster when his front brake locked up and he crashed. He was out of motor cycle racing for several months, but later went on to make his name with Velocettes. The 1948 Senior TT looked very promising for Moto Guzzi, with Omobono Tenni leading the race on his 500 twin – but he crashed into a wall. But all was not lost for the Mandello bikes, as Maurice Cann snatched victory in the lightweight event, then went on to take three World Championships between 1949 and 1952 with the single-cylinder 250. This machine scored magnificently in 1952, taking a 1–2–3 at that year's Lightweight TT. The closest Moto Guzzi came to a Senior TT win in the postwar years was in 1955, when Ken Kavanagh finished third overall.

The other thing that returned to Italy with the postwar peace was a desire to go racing again. Revived from prewar days, the 250cc Albatros was improved in a number of minor ways. The fuel tank was a little larger and of a different shape. The oil tank was also modified and, of course, this example is devoid of all road electrics even to the extent of no dynamo being fitted. This beautiful little machine continued to be offered to clubmen until 1949, when the Gambalunghino was introduced.

If the 1946 Dondolino looks remarkably like the Albatros, it's no coincidence, for the frame has its roots in the smaller-engined machine. Like the Albatros, the Dondolino was a production racer for amateur use, fitted with the pushrod valve big single engine. The engine now had higher compression, a larger (35mm throat) carburettor and modified valve timing. The result was a power output of 33bhp at 5500rpm and a top speed of almost 110mph. The Dondolino was available until 1951.

e factory twin-cylinder racers were revived after the war, too, and performed well. This 1947 edition survives the Moto Guzzi museum and has not been specially prepared, other than cleaned, for display. This is how it)ked at the end of its racing career. The Bicilindrica is thought by many to have been the absolute epitome of izzi's greatest machines.

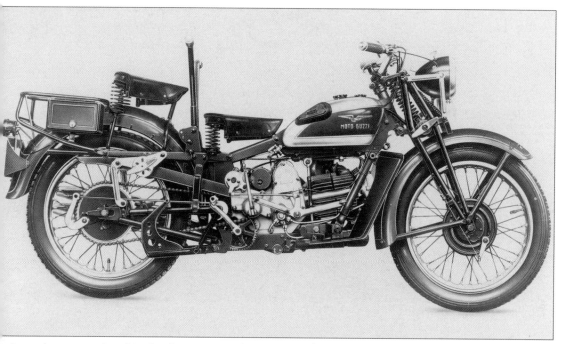

e Superalce was produced in this form in 1946 for public utility use, such as the armed forces and police. This del retains the prewar girder forks at the front and friction shock absorbers to the rear. While the pannier me at the back carries only lightweight toolboxes in this picture, it is clearly substantial enough to carry a ch heavier load. The Superalce continued in production until 1957. This example, with chromed accessories, learly a Carabinieri version, which would have had light olive green paintwork.

The Motocarrozzino GTV also continued in production after the war and this 1947 example shows the elegant sidecar to good advantage. Note also the very substantial sidecar chassis and attachment. The telescopic front forks, deep front mudguard and well-cowled sidecar wheel are all visible here, in a very functional outfit.

Miniaturisation of motor cycles had never been on Moto Guzzi's agenda before, but circumstances were different now. Italy had recently emerged from the most ravaging war in its history; the country had no natural reserves of its own and vehicle taxation now clearly favoured small engine displacements – which is why the 6 two-stroke Motoleggera was introduced in 1946. It was cheap and simple to make, with a single backbone frame and a diminutive engine producing just 2bhp, which was enough to propel the machine along Italian streets 30mph. Most significantly, the average fuel consumption was an incredible 140+ mpg and the machine loo like a proper motor cycle. This is a 1948 example.

ack on the track, Guzzi decided to explore further its new-found knowledge of small engine technology by
reating a parallel twin racer. The new Due Cilindri 250 appeared in 1947, inspired by the 1939 Three Cylinder.
his new design featured dual overhead camshafts and made extensive use of light alloys. The output was 25bhp
nd the top speed was over 100mph. However, it was bigger than the Albatros and its handling was not as good
s that of the single-cylinder machine, and as a consequence the Due Cilindri was dropped by the end of 1948
nd development efforts refocused on the single-cylinder.

he GTW was the final development of the GT line of machines. This one is a 1947 machine, with light alloy
vheels and sporty handlebars. The deeper mudguards of the revived GTV were also used on this GTW, as well as
mproved brakes and suspension. The slightly larger carburettor gave a better fuel range and allowed the engine
o propel the motor cycle at over 80mph. Finished in red, with liberal applications of chrome, it was an attractive
00cc tourer.

The postwar Airone was also 'given the treatment' and by 1948 had the same kind of deeper mudguards as th larger machines. It was equipped with Guzzi-designed telescopic forks and now had fully enclosed valve gear o the engine. This version still has the chromed fuel tank with painted side panels. That would change before lon; but this was the Airone of the time, capable of taking its rider up to 75mph. Pretty good for a 250!

Riding a Motoleggera with minimal streamlining and wheel discs, Raffaele Alberti set four new 75cc Class spee records on 2 February 1948. He took the Standing Kilometre at 71.705km/h, the Flying Kilometre a 95.051km/h, the Standing Mile at 79.554km/h and the Flying Mile at 96.072km/h. Later in the same yea some twenty-seven new records were taken, from 1km to 1,000km. Even in a high state of tune, the engine wa only giving 3.6bhp, so these records were all the more remarkable.

he year 1948 was an important one for
oto Guzzi, as its racing calendar was very
ll. The racing Bicilindrica now had a new
ame designed by Antonio Micucci, and a
uch shorter, squat appearance. This
irposeful-looking machine was taken to the
le of Man by Omobono Tenni for an attack
n the Senior TT. Sadly, he was plagued with
nition problems, but even so he set a new
p record at 88mph. It was to be his last
ce.

mobono Tenni was described as perhaps the
ravest and most determined racer of his time at
oto Guzzi: a natural winner. The 1948 Isle of
an TT was Tenni's last race. In practice at
remgarten, in Switzerland, for the European
rand Prix – a meeting for cars and motor cycles
he went out on to the circuit on practice day in
eavy rain. When he failed to return to the pits,
ews went out to find him; they discovered his
dy at the side of the track, with his 250 Due
lindri on the other side. Nobody knows exactly
w he died. Soon afterwards, the great Achille
arzi went out to test his Tipo 158 Alfetta car in
milar weather conditions. Rounding a bend,
arzi dropped a front wheel on to the verge. The
ir somersaulted and rolled over, crushing his
cull. Two of Italy's greatest racers had met their
d on the same day and in the same way.

One of the most attractive versions of the 500cc Bicilindrica is this 1949 example, with the fuel-tank fairing running ahead of the forks and handlebars. The carburettor to the rear cylinder is very close to the rear wheel. This complicated-looking machine, with its leading link forks so characteristic of this and later racing Guzzis, won the 1949 Italian Championship ridden by Enrico Lorenzetti.

The most successful racing 500 engine of its time was Moto Guzzi's Bicilindrica. This is a late example and the deep finning on the horizontal cylinder is clearly visible. Note also the beautifully machined crankshaft and the skew gear drives to the overhead camshafts. The gear cluster can be seen above the normally finned upper cylinder. On the opposite side of the picture are the hairpin valve springs. All this came together to produce a motor cycle capable of speeds up to 140mph.

The 500cc Gambalunga was the next step along the racing development road for Moto Guzzi. This was the 1949 version with the deeper inverted tray-type rear mudguard. Note also the leading link telescopic front forks and the rider-adjustable friction-type shock absorber for the rear wheel. The Gambalunga was primarily intended for works riders, though a very small number did reach privateers. It was favoured for a time over the Bicilindrica, because of its better handling on tight circuits.

y 1950 the 500cc Astore looked like this. It was in effect a serious update of the GTV which, by the time the esigners had finished with it, had become a new motor cycle. It was a thoroughly modern motor cycle in its day nd was very popular among touring enthusiasts. The engine featured fully enclosed valve gear and was coupled) a four-speed foot-change gearbox.

his piece of motor-cycling frivolity was created by Guzzi dealer and former racer Rino Berton. The event was a elebration of Holy Year in Rome during 1950 and Berton was playing the part of a Roman charioteer. His chariot' was created from three Motoleggera 65s coupled together with a couple of 'sidecars' between them. The eins of the chariot operated the controls. The device was built in 1949 and was first shown at a major Moto iuzzi rally in that year.

Bruno Ruffo (no. 1) lines up for the start of the Nations Grand Prix at Monza in 1949 with a 250cc Gambalunghino. In that same year Ruffo brought Moto Guzzi their first world title: the 250cc Championship. The Gambalunghino might never have come into existence had it not been for Enrico Lorenzetti deciding to repair his race-damaged Albatros by fitting the mechanical components into a Gambalunga frame. Thus was born the 250cc Gambalunga – the Gambalunghino.

Frivolity aside, the Motoleggera was the most prolific Guzzi model, accounting for the largest number of motor cycles made at Mandello del Lario. But the commercial side of the business did well, too, and the 500cc Erco had a long production run of almost nine years from 1950. This version has the regular wooden body and a dis front wheel.

Ercole Motocarros in the dispatch hall at Mandello. These machines accounted for a substantial chunk of Mot Guzzi's revenue in their eight-year production life. The fact that this batch is unbodied suggests that they ma have left the factory in that state – they may have been military examples to be bodied elsewhere, or perhaps the were simply awaiting movement to a bodyshop for the installation of bodies before delivery.

houghts had been entertained at Mandello del Lario of retiring the 120-degree V-twin Bicilindrica from front
he racing, but the Gambalunga, while fine on twisty road circuits, just wasn't up to the faster grand prix-style
ents. So, with the anatomically shaped tank, a longer single-seat pad, a deeper rear mudguard and slightly
odified exhaust pipes, the old faithful twin continued in service. Bob Foster rode one in the 1950 Senior TT, but
hole appeared in one of the carburettor induction tubes, causing the engine to misfire badly, and he was forced
retire while lying in sixth place.

he motor scooter was beginning to catch on all over Europe in the late 1940s. Moto Guzzi's answer to this
allenge, having already taken the world by storm with the Motoleggera, was the Galletto ('Cockerel'). The
alletto was half motor cycle and half scooter and with its larger-than-average scooter-sized engine of 160cc, it
as endowed with a much-better-than-average scooter performance. This new machine offered the 'step-through'
cility of the scooter, but with its larger wheels was able to retain much of the handling of a motor cycle. The
ont-mounted spare wheel was a particularly novel feature and the Galletto quickly became very popular.

Back on the racing scene, the Gambalunghino came in for quite a lot of attention for the 1951 season. This wa the type on which Bruno Ruffo had secured the first 250cc world championship in 1949. In 1950 th Gambalunghino didn't do so well, winning only one grand prix, so for 1951 it received the revamp whic produced this machine. A faired rear seat/mudguard made it look a bit faster and red paint (instead of silve made it look more 'Guzzi'. Tommy Wood won the 1951 Junior TT on a Gambalunghino, but it didn't have as lon a record of success that year as its designers had hoped.

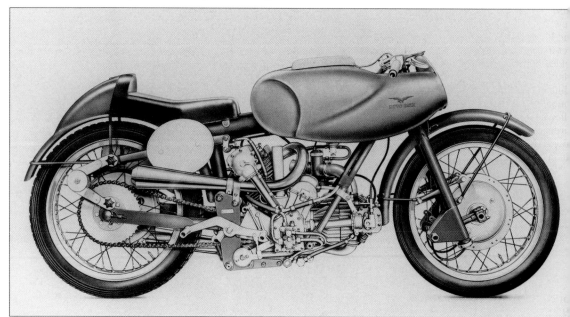

The final version of the Bicilindrica came in 1951. Retaining the anatomical fuel tank, this final version adopte the same rider's saddle as the Gambalunghino. Hartford-type friction rear shock absorbers were revived for th model, in preference to the earlier underslung hydraulic type and the engine was further 'tweaked' to produc 47bhp. However, the design was showing its age by now and other makers were beating the Guzzi more often, s the Bicilindrica's swansong was really the very wet Swiss Grand Prix, won by Fergus Anderson at the amazin speed of 80.16mph. Anderson was followed into third place by Enrico Lorenzetti on a similar machine.

The anatomical fuel tank used on the
Bicilindrica of 1951 was carried over to the
Gambalunghino in the following year. This
view suggests the Gambalunghino was longer
and lower than its larger-engined sibling – in
fact it was lower, but not longer. Moto Guzzi
fielded only the Gambalunghino in 1952,
winning five Grands Prix, including the Manx,
while Fergus Anderson made it a Manx
double by also winning the Lightweight TT,
followed into second place by Enrico
Lorenzetti and third by Bruno Ruffo (who
slowed down to let the other two through on
the last lap, in accordance with team orders).

Enrico Lorenzetti just beat Fergus Anderson to the
1952 250cc World Championship and spent a
great deal of his time, when not racing, doing test
and development work. This picture shows him in
1953, astride a Bialbero with a rather battered
'bird-beak' fairing (the 'bird-beak' being the front
mudguard), upon which he won the 250cc
Siracusa Grand Prix.

Back in the world of making motor cycles to pay the bills, Moto Guzzi had now developed the Airone into a ver elegant machine for its day. The Airone Sport was a 250cc 'real motor cycle', with a healthy performance match its good looks. There was a pillion seat, but to keep the sporting appearance and character a rear seat pa was fitted, like that of the earlier racers.

The 250cc engine of the Airone was a tidy and businesslike assembly. Note the fully enclosed valve gear, th characteristic right-angle curved inlet manifold with the Dell'Orto carburettor pointing out slightly to pick up co air. The usual tight layout of engine, gearbox and ancillaries typified the best of horizontal Guzzi design.

Preserving the family identity was the Airone's larger sibling, the Falcone, pictured here in 'Sport' form. Only by looking at the two machines side by side can you tell them apart. Clearly the engine of the Falcone is bigger, being a 500, while at the rear the manually adjustable friction shock absorber is also a giveaway on the larger machine. But the family resemblance was deliberately very strong.

Fergus Anderson was a brilliant rider and won many races for Moto Guzzi, including an amazing forty-six grand prix events. He was also the first Scotsman to win the 350cc World Championship, a traditional arena of the British bike makers, especially Norton and AJS. That was in 1953, when he was forty-four. In the preceding year, he had won the Junior TT – becoming the oldest man to do so.

The amazing in-line Quattro Cilindri (Four Cylinder) was not a Carcano design, but the work of Carlo Gianini, an engineer from Rome who was brought in by Giorgio Parodi specifically to produce a competitive successor to Giulio Carcano's Bicilindrica. It was a purposeful-looking machine and on occasions proved very fast. But unreliability plagued it from the beginning and it was not an easy ride, so it was not popular with riders. It won only one significant event, at Hockenheim, in the hands of Lorenzetti, and just over a year later it was abandoned.

Small motor cycles still paid the profits of Moto Guzzi in the early and mid-1950s. For simplicity and economy, two-stroke engines were preferred by most manufacturers, including Guzzi. The Zigolo was introduced in 1953 to bridge the gap between the Motoleggera 65 and the Galletto. Originally fitted with a 98cc engine, this publicity shot shows the Zigolo Lusso, with part-chromed fuel tank and brightwork around the engine. It was a pretty machine and had a long life, growing to 110cc by 1966, its final year.

Still using the 65cc engine, the Cardellino was essentially a revamp of the Motoleggera. Introduced in 1954, the Cardellino was a result of manufacturing cost reductions aimed at holding on to the drifting market. A number of changes were made during its eleven-year life, including an engine size increase to 73cc in 1956 and another step up to 83cc in 1962. By 1965 demand had fallen to a level which could no longer sustain production, so the little 'Guzzino' was withdrawn.

CHAPTER SEVEN

PROGRESS AND CONSOLIDATION ON ROAD AND TRACK

Moto Guzzi's 350cc single was created to mount a challenge to the dominant British AJS and Norton racers in that class. It had begun life as a 'stretched' Gambalunghino engine, enlarged to its limit of 317cc. So successful was that original creation that the design team went to work to make it into a 345cc unit. With only 35bhp to its credit, it was the aerodynamic efficiency of the 'dustbin' fairing, developed in Moto Guzzi's own wind tunnel, that gave it a top speed of over 135mph. The 350 gave Guzzi four consecutive World Championships, in 1954, 1955, 1956 and 1957.

A key feature of Moto Guzzi's great success in the 1950s was the company's decision to participate in 350cc racing. This venture began in 1953, with a developed version of the Gambalunghino – the Bialbero, which became very successful. This was a single-cylinder, twin-cam-engined machine, using Gambalungino cycle parts and a new fuel-tank. The new fairing (developed with the benefit of testing in the new wind-tunnel installed at Mandello) extended to cover the front mudguard and quickly became known as the 'bird-beak' fairing (for obvious reasons). Coupled to the twin-cam engine was a five-speed gearbox.

The most successful rider of these motor cycles was the Englishman Fergus Anderson. Born in 1909, Anderson had been well known as a motor cycle racer before the Second World War, but astride Moto Guzzis he reached the pinnacle of his career, with wins in the Swiss Grand Prix of 1950 and 1951, and Lightweight TT wins in 1952 and 1953. He later became racing manager at Mandello del Lario and furthered the careers of Bill Lomas, Ken Kavanagh and Duilio Agostini. He established a fine reputation as both an outstanding rider and a skilled technician, whose riding experience enabled him to evaluate modifications and design improvements.

As the 1954 racing season opened, Moto Guzzi brought streamlined fairings up to date by integrating them into the overall design of their motor cycles; the frames were now of the 'trellis' type, extending over and around the front wheel to support the all-enveloping 'dustbin' fairing. The tremendous success of these aerodynamic machines, tested for effect in the Mandello wind tunnel, was instantaneous and their design was quickly copied by the competition. The 350 Guzzi was able to turn in the remarkable fuel consumption of almost 56 miles per gallon, which was a very important factor in long-distance race strategy. The company was now spending huge sums on racing and victory was an essential return on its investment. The single-cylinder 500, with its classic 88 x 82mm bore and stroke, was still winning races, while the 350 took four world championships between 1953 and 1956: Fergus Anderson took the first two, Ken Kavanagh won the Junior TT of 1955 and Bill Lomas won the 1956 TT.

Late in 1953 it was decided that the Quattro Cilindri in-line four was not going to win as many races as Moto Guzzi wanted, so a totally new machine emerged from the drawing-board and was built in prototype form before the year was out. Umberto Todero described this – the immortal V8 machine ridden with great skill by Bill Lomas and Dickie Dale – to the author as the most exciting motor cycle ever built at Mandello del Lario. The V8 was a mechanical marvel which was years ahead of its time. The in-line Four, with its longitudinal position in the frame, orthodox gearbox and shaft drive, was not a successful racer, so the engineering team went back to their drawing-boards to design the optimum power unit for their next racing motor cycle. The decision to go fo an Eight rested on dimensional acceptability and balance: a transverse V8 could be built within a maximum width of 50cm, and with a 90-degree angle between the cylinder blocks the weight distribution would be much the same as on a single-cylinder machine.

Moto Guzzi's Otto Cilindri was perhaps the most charismatic motor cycle of all time, including the most exotic modern examples from Japan. In fact, it was only a little more successful than its four-cylinder predecessor, but it had all the ingredients of a truly great motor cycle. If only Moto Guzzi had persevered with it, and indeed with racing. But it was not to be. The V-8 Guzzi had raced in numerous major events, including the Tourist Trophy, and throughout 1956 the 500 V-8 continued to be developed, but the decision of the major Italian motor cycle manufacturers to withdraw from road racing brought its career to a premature end. (The withdrawal from racing was very largely a consequence of the ban on 'dustbin' fairings, which was imposed after investigations into an accident concluded that the steering was impaired by their presence.)

You could be forgiven for asking how Moto Guzzi found time to manufacture motor cycles for sale to the public, but they did. On the commercial front, the Motocarro was selling in substantial numbers, and providing Italy with a pool of lightweight low-cost transport. (It's amazing just how many you can still see on Italian streets today!) The Falcone 500 was now at the peak of its success, and it was accompanied by the 247cc Airone, the 175cc Lodola lightweight, as well as the smaller Zigolo, which came along later. The Airone was a particular success story, being the most popular single-cylinder machine in the Guzzi range for most of its nine-year production life. Of course, every motor cycle has its limits and the Airone reached the end of its useful life in 1959, to be succeeded by the 235cc version of the Lodola.

There was something for everyone here, in a high-quality product range that embraced lightweight novice machines up to world-beating international long-distance road racers and grand prix winners. The company left the 1950s on a high note, with a string of significant racing successes, a thoroughly popular range of production machines and the legendary 500cc V8.

A former Norton rider, Australian Ken Kavanagh joined Moto Guzzi in 1954. He rode 500s and the 350 with some notable successes, perhaps the most significant of which was the 1956 Junior TT. Here, he's riding a 350 twin cam in typical 'on the limit' style. Kavanagh was Guzzi's principal tester and also took part in a record run

...Cavanagh, su Moto Gurri 350 cc.

...t Montlhery in March 1955, to set new 8, 9 and 10 hour and 1,000 mile records for the 350cc, 500cc, 750cc
...nd 1000cc classes.

The 'Three Musketeers' of Moto Guzzi's design squad were Giulio Cesare Carcano (left), Enrico Cantoni and Umberto Todero (right). Under Carcano's leadership, the development of Moto Guzzi motor cycles ensured they stayed at the top in racing right to the end. By 1957, when Moto Guzzi withdrew from first-class competition, they had to their credit 14 world championships and 47 Italian championships, and had notched up no fewer than 3,329 race wins since 1921. Giulio Carcano and his team were responsible for a very large chunk of that success between 1937 and 1957.

Between 1955 and 1957 Moto Guzzi worked on the most outstanding racing motor cycle design of all time. The brainchild of Giulio Carcano, the Otto Cilindri – the magnificent V8 500 – was, and still is, a legend. It is shown here with its 'dustbin' fairing, the design which caused so much trouble in 1957 that a whole group of manufacturers withdrew from racing when it was banned. The V8 design was simply too far ahead of its time in terms of frame development and tyre technology, and it proved to be a difficult machine to ride.

This drawing by the author shows the Otto Cilindri without the fairing and exposes the transverse 90-degree V engine. There was much boardroom debate about the development of this engine at Moto Guzzi, and for the first time Carlo Guzzi found himself overruled when he expressed the preference to develop a single before progressing to the V8. But Enrico Parodi was anxious to progress and so the Otto Cilindri was built.

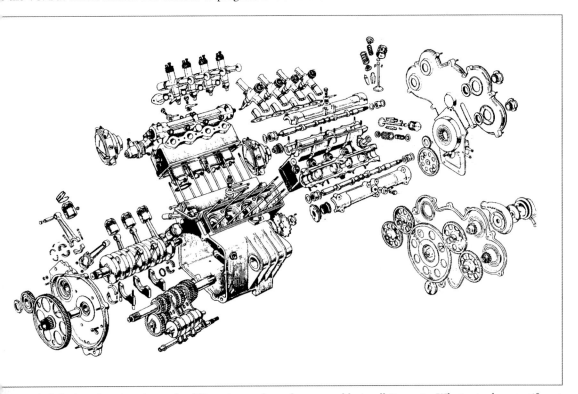

This exploded view drawing shows the V8 engine and gearbox assembly in all its parts. What a truly magnificent creation. This is the first version, with the six-speed gearbox and carburettors with no individual float chambers. The crankshaft and valve gear were also modified as the machine developed through its two-year life. In its ultimate form this engine propelled the Guzzi V8 to an amazing top speed of 172mph.

With all the racing development going on, there seemed little time for production engineering at Mandello de Lario. However, the 192cc engine from the Galletto was adapted to a lightweight goods carrier, below the weight and class of the 500cc Ercole Motocarro. This resulted in the Ercolino, a 192cc three-wheeler ideal for moving small loads around narrow small town streets. This was a shaft-driven vehicle, and the one shown here is a 1959 version with smaller road wheels. A cab was also available as an option. This little machine was produced up to 1970.

Moto Guzzi's Lodola was the first single-cylinder motor cycle to move away from the traditional horizontal engine position. Sporty 175s were the fashion in the mid-1950s and this new machine was launched in 1956 to meet that demand. Fitted with a chain-driven single overhead camshaft, the chain had a novel spring-loaded tensioner to keep the chain tight. This was the last machine to be designed entirely by Carlo Guzzi and was a popular machine, being produced for ten years.

y 1959 Carlo Guzzi's Lodola engine had expanded to 235cc in the GT version, seen here. The hooded headlamp, cript 'Gran Turismo' and slightly beefier appearance were the tell-tale signs of the GT over the Normale version. wasn't a particularly fast machine, but could touch close to 80mph. Altogether almost 27,000 Lodolas were uilt between 1956 and 1966.

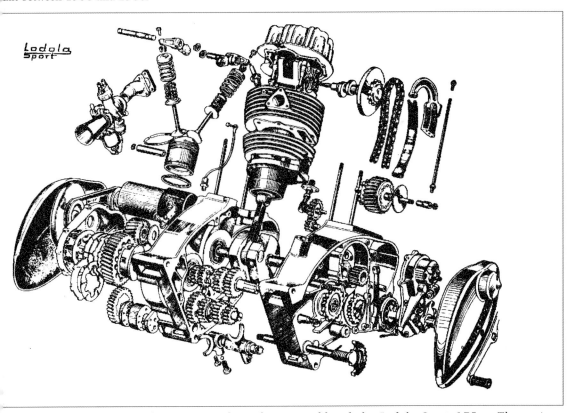

his exploded view shows the engine and gearbox assembly of the Lodola Sport 175cc. The various haracteristics of this new Carlo Guzzi-designed engine are clear to see, including Guzzi's timing chain tensioner, he inclined overhead valves and the four-speed gearbox. It was no longer a 'flat' engine assembly.

CHAPTER EIGHT

DEVELOPING A MARKET WITHOUT RACING

The Zigolo was improved by adding a redesigned fuel tank and a 110cc engine, along with telescopic forks, a new front hub and telescopic rear shock absorbers. The general bodywork was basically the same as the original design, but the machine looked generally more modern. The exhaust consisted of a front pipe, a seam-welded box silencer and a small bore outlet pipe. Generally, as in the preceding generation of Guzzis, this new Zigolo bore a strong family resemblance to the Lodola, its larger sibling.

The Milan Show of November 1959 gave Moto Guzzi the opportunity to show the world what it could offer for the new decade. But there was no sign of a racing machine. World class racing was a thing of the past for the Mandello firm, though clearly the company's racing record was too good a marketing tool to ignore, while the Otto Cilindri 500 was still firmly in the minds of those enthusiasts who thought that Moto Guzzi should not have abandoned racing altogether. But racing was finished, and the future would carry a different message: that of solid reliability and economy.

Like most Italian motor cycle manufacturers at the time, Moto Guzzi entered the 1960s with a degree of trepidation. Enrico Parodi had foreseen that the entry level market was the most important sector to nurture, providing cheap basic transport to a wide spectrum of customers, and so the plan for the 1960s was focused around this end of the market. The little 98cc Zigolo had joined the 65cc Cardellino in the mid-1950s, and the Galletto scooter had proved popular, so 1960 saw the introduction of the 192cc version of this 'scootercycle'. The Cardellino was offered in two versions, the basic Turismo and the Lusso. From 1958, it had acquired an 83cc engine, having grown from 65cc to 73cc in the 1950s.

The Zigolo appeared in 1953 and was so well received that in its first year of production it sold over 6,000 examples. The panelled-in framework of the Lusso, introduced a year later, made the Zigolo look a more solid machine altogether and thus much more acceptable to the youngster who wanted a bigger motor cycle but couldn't afford one (today, it's called 'street cred'). The last version of the Zigolo was actually launched in 1959 and went on show in Milan that year. It now featured a 110cc engine, with a square bore/stroke configuration of 52 x 52mm, and over 12,000 were sold in 1960.

The Lodola came into the 1960s as a 235cc machine, displacing the Airone as the 'Quarter-Litre' Moto Guzzi. The original 175cc version had a chain-driven overhead camshaft, and the Sport version's engine produced 11bhp (although this wasn't powerful enough to take on the likes of Ducati or Mondial). So the 235 was created, but now with a pushrod overhead valve engine, so making it less costly to manufacture and helping to keep the price down. The Lodola looked like a real motor cycle – and it looked like a true Guzzi, too, though a few of its characteristics were novel. For example, its engine was angled at 45 degrees and there was a bit more panelwork around. Dry sump lubrication continued to be standard and a four-speed gearbox was now fitted to the machine. While never credited with a particularly sporting performance, the Lodola did quickly gain a reputation for being a solid, reliable means of transport.

Times were changing by 1960, as indicated in the range of motor cycles available from Moto Guzzi. The market had taken a dip as Mandello del Lario's new 1960 product line was announced but the company had correctly anticipated the way forward. For some time Moto Guzzi had been focusing more attention on the junior market, so the announcement of the Stornello, which was simply following the trend already established, also allowed the company to meet the market problems head on with a new small commuter/beginner machine.

Giulio Carcano was responsible for the Stornello's design. It was a cleverly created lightweight machine of stylish appearance. Carcano had excelled in the design of racers, but this little 125 showed very convincingly that he was also eminently capable of producing a low cost (to manufacture, that is) highly functional motor cycle, with a number of new features. For example, the engine was tilted forward 25 degrees, the engine/gearbox unit worked as a stressed member in the duplex frame and the crankcase halves were pressure die castings. The power unit was a pushrod overhead valve device, with the valves parallel mounted. Lubrication was from a wet sump and ignition from a flywheel-mounted magneto. The neat little engine and gearbox unit had two bolt holes in the crankcase at the front end and another at the rear, which allowed it to be bolted into the frame, filling the gap between the front and rear sections of the frame, so making it a stressed member of the chassis structure. (This was not a new idea, for a number of the world's very early motor-bicycle makers had used the same principle in the construction of their machines in the early days of the twentieth century, placing the engine alone between front and rear frame members, though 'stressed member' would hardly qualify as a description at that time.)

Carcano's clever design produced a small motor cycle that was flexible, durable and inexpensive. Inevitably a Sport version appeared not long after its introduction, in 1961. This model's engine had inclined valves, a feature designed to improve its performance from the standard 7hp. The Stornello's success can be judged by the fact that it was ultimately offered in Touring, Sport, Scrambler and Regolarita versions. In its sixteen-year life (1960–75), it acquired a five-speed gearbox option and inherited a larger (160cc) engine. The Stornello was one of Moto Guzzi's best sellers.

his was the final version of the Galletto 192, photographed in 1961. A version with rear side panniers and a ﾑall top box in place of the pillion seat was produced in quantity for the Italian postal service. This was the first oto Guzzi to be offered with electric starting and the model continued in production until 1966. It was offered ﾑished in either grey or Guzzi Red.

e Stornello was introduced in 1960 and looked like a scaled-down Lodola. The 125cc engine even resembled a ﾑall Lodola unit, though it was a dual pushrod design. The machine was designed to bring down the price of ﾑtor-cycling, being cheap to produce. This is the Sport version which was capable of around 70mph and ﾑtainly looked the part. The Stornello was built in Turismo, Sport and Scrambler (Regolarita) versions.

Having abandoned circuit and road racing, Moto Guzzi took an interest in trialling and the Regolarita version of the Lodola, in 235cc engine form, proved to be highly successful. First entered in trials events in 1958, Lodolas were eventually developed to a level where they took four gold medals in the 1959 International Six Days Trial held that year at Gottwaldov in Czechoslovakia. It was a very successful competitor at a fraction of the cost of the racing programme of the 1950s.

Utility vehicles were still considered important to the reputation and earning power of Moto Guzzi, so in 1962 the Zigolo 110-engined Aiace Motocarro, complete with fully enclosed driver's cab, came on to the market. Handlebar-steered, it came with a variety of bodies, including this box van design. Again aimed at lightweight work in narrow streets, it was quite successful and sold moderately well.

versatility was always a hallmark
of Guzzi design, but who could
have imagined that a lightweight
mechanical plough would find its
way into the Moto Guzzi catalogue
in the early 1960s? The Motozappa
was very similar to the Rotavator
offered in the British market.
Primarily a cultivator for use in
large private gardens or by small-
scale commercial growers, it could
plough or level out ground
prepared for cultivation. The power
came from the Dingo 49cc two-
stroke and the Motozappa proved a
popular tool.

As well as the Motozappa, Moto
Guzzi made other lightweight
tools for tilling the land. This one,
actually heavier than the 'Zappa',
is the Motocoltivatore. This was a
device for preparing land for
sowing small market-gardens.
Small agricultural tractors didn't
exist then, nor the tools they
would have required, and this
was the way that the small-holder
mechanised his activities.

A larger version of the Motozappa
was made with the Zigolo 110cc
engine. This version was more
than just a lightweight cultivator
– it also had a load-carrying
body. It accommodated its driver
in motor cycle fashion and was
handlebar-steered. The single
backbone chassis had footrests
mounted to it, and also the
handbrake lever. The engine had
no cowling and the whole
structure looked pretty crude in
comparison with Moto Guzzi's
motor cycles, but in 1965 getting
the job done was more important
than looking good.

CHAPTER NINE

TOWARDS A NEW ERA

In 1963 a new lightweight arrived on the scene from Mandello del Lario. At first glance, the Dingo was not a particularly imposing design, as a near step-through 50cc. However, even the Turismo (or Tre Marce – Three Speed) did well, as it was relatively cheap and was well suited to the economy and youth markets. It was launched in the midst of a crisis in the market and with its small engine, easy ride and three-speed gearbox it proved to be a good seller. This is a 1967 model, not drastically changed from the original.

The early 1960s was a period of great trial for Moto Guzzi, in that the company was facing boardroom wrangles and the product line was competing for a shrinking market. By 1963, realising that they needed to produce something less expensive than the existing models for the lower end of the market, the Mandello management bought up a stock of mopeds from a small struggling firm in Milan while the Moto Guzzi designers went to work on the next product in the range – the Dingo.

Typically, the Dingo didn't remain a simple moped for long, though the original model did have pedals. It was powered by a 50cc two-stroke engine which passed its modest power through a three-speed gearbox and this new machine was launched in 1963 at the Milan Trade Fair. The Dingo was a success and did attract new customers, as a result of which there was soon a Dingo Sport on the market, with a four-speed gearbox. Later in the machine's development, a Super Sport came on to the scene – and a very sporty-looking little machine it was, too. By the end of its production life, the Dingo was being offered in economy form with an automatic gearbox, appealing directly to the commuter.

Despite all the model development that went on at Moto Guzzi, the company still had serious problems. The factory, although in a beautiful location at the foot of Mount Grigna, was limited in its growth potential and was of an outdated design. There wasn't enough money in reserve to rebuild, so the structure remained as it was. The machine tools were outdated and becoming unreliable, showing their age by breaking down at inconvenient times. The company really needed to be operating on a much larger scale if it was to be a major league player.

At the beginning of 1966 the financial state of Moto Guzzi was such that the board of directors found it necessary to put the company into receivership. An administrator was appointed, who operated the business for some time until it was decided that the state enterprise organisation, SEIMM, would take over and run it until a buyer could be found. The government was reluctant to let the company slide into obscurity and so, as it had done at Alfa Romeo in Milan some thirty years before, it stepped in to manage the company. The plan was to reverse the company's fortunes, so that it could be sold on as a going concern. (SEIMM – 'Societa Esercizio Indusriale Moto Mecchaniche – was established as a division of the Istituto Mobiliare Italiano, the state body created to rescue and run organisations regarded as important to the nation's prestige, mostly temporarily, but sometimes long term. It followed the pattern of Mussolini's pre-war Istituto Ricostruzione Italiano).

The company was now very different. Both Giorgio Parodi and Carlo Guzzi were gone, and the state management board consisted of many new faces, most of whom were wholly unfamiliar with the motor cycle manufacturing industry. It was fortunate, then, that such loyal stalwarts as Giulio Carcano and Umberto Todero had stayed at their beloved company long enough to produce the next generation of Moto Guzzi machines – the immortal shaft-drive V-twins that are so familiar today. Sadly, Carcano and his principal assistant Enrico Cantoni were casualties of the reorganisation. Giulio Carcano has never talked about his departure from Moto Guzzi, but it is perhaps sufficient to say that he never worked on another motor cycle design project again, moving over to the design of boats instead.

The V7 was the first of the long line of transverse V-twin-engined Moto Guzzis, but it was not the first V-twin-engined Guzzi machine. That distinction is held by what might be described as the most unlikely vehicle you could imagine: a three-wheeled (or rather one-wheeled and two-tracked) machine developed specifically for the Italian Army's Alpine regiments. The military specification called for a lightweight cargo vehicle capable of carrying 500kg across rough terrain. It had to be able to climb Alpine gradients with a driver and full load without difficulty.

Moto Guzzi's response to this challenge was a total redesign of the Motocarro concept. It had three-wheel-drive to begin with and was powered by a Carcano-designed air-cooled four-stroke V-twin engine of 754cc displacement. This was mounted with the crankshaft in the longitudinal plane, driving a six-speed gearbox, which transmitted power to the rear wheels by means of a driveshaft. There are pictures of it climbing up walls, which illustrate the tremendous versatility of the beast. While this fantastic little military vehicle, known colloquially as the 'Mechanical Mule', didn't get past the development stage into volume production, some 220 were built, including the prototypes, and they left their mark in the driveline concept adopted for all future large Moto Guzzi motor cycles. It is still the driveline pattern used today.

The V7 was a 704cc grand tourer aimed specifically at the quality end of the big motor cycle market. Its principal advantage over the big twins of BMW lay in its V-twin of 90 degrees – the BMW engines were flat-twins ('boxer' engines) with all their inherent problems. The Guzzi's engine was never likely to foul on the road surface, though the designer had to ensure that the rider's legs were well out of the way to avoid a scorching.

Developments of the V7 led to a healthy market for Moto Guzzi in the public sector where, for example, the highway police bought large numbers, as did other public authorities. Moto Guzzi had been famous for its service to its country, supplying machines for many years to military and civil authorities since the 1920s. The public sector was now to be its best market for some time, which was sufficient to attract the attention of Alejandro de Tomaso, whose influence would soon take the company out of SEIMM ownership and back into the private sector.

Giulio Carcano's V-twin engine design was originally produced as an idea for a motor cycle, but the company was not yet ready to embark on a large-engined two-wheeler, so it was suggested as a power unit for the Fiat 500 car. A prototype engine was built and fitted to a Fiat gearbox. The engine and gearbox fitted well into the car's engine compartment and the capacity of the power unit was increased during its development to 650cc. But it came to nothing, until a government tender was issued for a military three-wheeled load-carrier.

In addition to the 'Mechanical Mule', a police specification was issued for a large-engined motor cycle, aimed essentially at replacing the Moto Guzzi 'Falcone'. This new machine would be required to run for 100,000km without major repairs and would be expected to keep pace with the kinds of cars now running on the autostradas. The result was ultimately the 850T3, a shaft-driven motor cycle which brought in its wake a long-lived and thoroughly enjoyable range of motor cycles, the magic of which remains with us to this day in some of the most exciting road machines that money can buy . . .

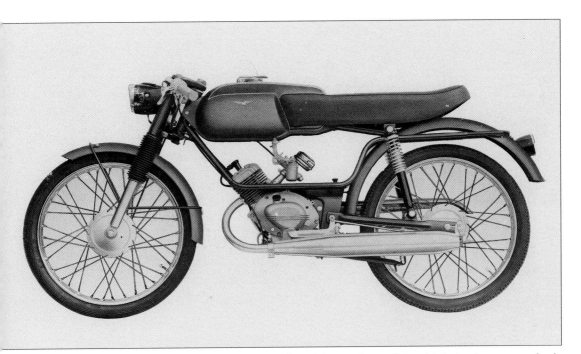

While the original Dingo Turismo had a fabricated pressed-steel frame, the traditional tubular frame came back with the Dingo Super and the other models in the Dingo range. Moto Guzzi recognised that young men wanted to ride something that looked like a real motor cycle, and preferably a sporting one at that, and the Dingo Super was produced to fit the bill. The engine and gearbox were mounted into sheet metalwork, as was the rear swinging arm. Even so, it looked like, and was, a sporty little machine.

The Dingo Cross followed the Super into the market place. Endowed with the same frame, tank and seat as the Super, the Cross had slightly different mudguards, higher handlebars that suited the motocross image and, of course, knobbly tyres. The exhaust was fitted with a perforated shield and was mounted high, also in keeping with the image. This example dates from 1967.

By 1966 the Stornello had achieved a following of its own and was still selling well. This is one of the late fir
series 125s, a Stornello 125 Turismo. It was not a particularly rapid machine, with a top speed of only arour
62mph, but it was a reliable commuter and light tourer, with attractive lines.

Still in 125cc form, the Stornello 125 Scrambler was announced in 1967. It was initially labelled 'Scramble
America' and partnered the 'Sport America', though a note from 1968 describes the machine illustrated here a
the 'Scrambler Italia'. It certainly looked the part, with good ground clearance, the high exhaust essential t
scrambling and even weight distribution. Note the later style cylinder head/rocker cover.

echnologically the most advanced Moto Guzzi creation since the 500cc V8 racer was the 3 x 3 all-terrain ilitary vehicle, known as the Mule. It was capable of carrying a payload of 500kg up slopes of 45 degrees. The hicle was designed by Giulio Carcano and the power unit was the V-twin (which led ultimately to the V7 igine). Fitted with a six-speed constant mesh gearbox, the low tune engine, which produced 20bhp, would most haul the vehicle up a wall.

nd here's a publicity shot of an Italian Alpine oldier taking his 3 x 3 literally up a wall. The ear tracks fitted over the tyres of the back heels and round the jockey wheels, making he Mule a virtual half-track. There were evelopment and stability problems with this achine, so only 220 were built between 1961 nd 1963.

Back on the commercial front, Moto Guzzi's love affair with its diminutive Dingo extended to the creation of another three-wheeled goods carrier. Chain-driven, this little three-wheeled truck looked like a motor scooter with a body attached. Low production costs didn't mean that it should be 'cheap', so telescopic front forks were considered important to providing a little rider/driver comfort, though the amount of pressed steel fabrication evident. The Dingotre appeared in 1965 and remained in production until 1968.

Moto Guzzi already had a tremendous reputation for making durable motor cycles but in 1967 they introduced the machine that would make everything else they had ever made look short-lived. The V7 was a 704cc V-twin developed from the power unit of the 3 x 3 Mule, and it was to influence Moto Guzzi development for more than thirty years. The example shown here is the 1967 V7 Corrazieri, the military/police version.

The civilian version of the V7 followed the Corrazieri and then in 1969 came the V7 Special. The machine seen here is the last version of the 700cc V7, which went on sale in 1968, just before the Special. This motor cycle did a great deal to revive interest in big machines. The sporting versions of the V7 were created from the V7 Special.

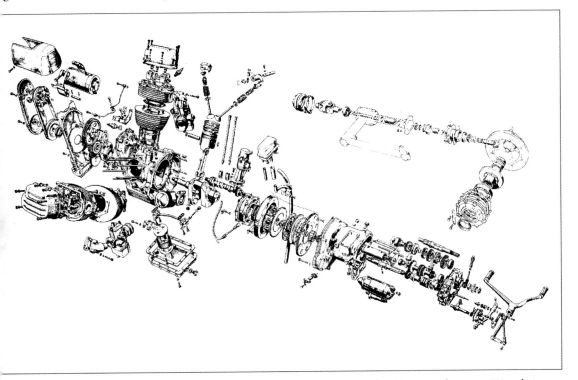

This cutaway drawing depicts the V7 Special engine and drivetrain. Note the 300 watt dynamo sitting between the cylinders – clearly the alternator had not yet become the universal way of providing electricity. The 60bhp power output, combined with a reduction in the motor cycle's weight of some 15kg, took the top speed of the V7 Special up to 115mph.

On 26 June 1969 two factory-prepared V7 Specials, fitted with 'dolphin'-style fairings, were taken to the Monza Autodrome to attack a series of international speed and distance records. One had a standard V7 Special engine of 757cc (left at that size to make an attempt on existing 1,000cc records, while the other's engine had a bore of only 82mm (instead of the standard 83mm) to bring its size down to 739.4cc, so allowing it to run for 750cc records. Both machines used standard V7 frames. Four riders went to Monza: Vittorio Brambilla, Guido Mandracci, Angelo Tenconi and Remo Venturi. Tyre problems robbed the team of any 1,000cc records, but the 100 Kilometre, the 1 Hour and the 1,000 Kilometre records in the 750cc class fell to Moto Guzzi at speeds between 128.7mph and 136.53mph.

Also in 1969 the Falcone Nuovo was developed for use by the armed forces and various police authorities. This is an early military version. Within a couple of years, the civilian variation of the new Falcone was also on offer, in response to popular demand. Note now that the 'bacon-slicer' flywheel has been fully enclosed.

While the Nuove Falcone was the biggest single in the Moto Guzzi range in 1969, the smallest-engined 'real motor cycle' was still the Dingo. Here's the Dingo Cross, looking every bit the 'teen-trials' machine. This is the version launched for the 1970 season, with lots of chrome and white paint to keep it in the fashion of the time.

CHAPTER TEN

MARKET DEVELOPMENT AND BACK TO THE TRACK

Still in the low cost end of the market, the 'shopper'-type of 'mini bike' was next to receive attention from Moto Guzzi. The power unit of the Trotter was even smaller, at 40cc, and it was basically a moped without pedals and could be used without vehicle registration and licence plates. Trotters like this 1964 example were (some still are) used as commuters by adults and young teenagers.

Moto Guzzi's racing days had ended in 1957, when the brilliant 'Otto Cilindri' V8 was abandoned. In common with most of the Italian motor cycle manufacturers, Moto Guzzi had decided to walk away from racing over a dispute with the organising authorities about the viability and safety of 'dustbin' fairings on racing machines. But a decade had passed now and Moto Guzzis had taken part, with great success, in the International Six Days Trial. So in 1969 a tentative step was taken into production bike racing, after the introduction of the V7 'Special' at that year's Milan show. Before moving into racing proper, though, a lightened version of the V7 Special was tuned up and fitted with a rudimentary fairing, and then taken to Monza Autodrome where it set new speed records in June and October for the 750cc and 1000cc classes.

Meanwhile the SEIMM management had been careful to preserve, as far as possible, Moto Guzzi's established identity, running the company very much on a 'business as usual' basis. Before SEIMM took over the reins at Mandello del Lario, the receiver and his team had looked closely at the economics of the product range and the structure of the factory and decided that the older models in the range, which now seemed to be less popular, should be discontinued. As a result, the Cardellino, Zigolo, Galletto and Lodola were all withdrawn from the catalogue in 1966 and the Falcone followed them a year later. Under SEIMM management, the Stornello would now be developed as the lightweight motor cycle in the range and the moped range would also be expanded, the Dingo being the flagship of that sector in Moto Guzzi's model line-up.

The Dingo had begun life as a pressed steel frame 50cc machine, and its Turismo version was aimed specifically at the youth and commuter markets. SEIMM's management team encouraged the development of the Sport and Super Sport versions, as they looked like miniature motor cycles and so would appeal to the youth market. Another Moto Guzzi moped was the Trotter, which had an even smaller engine than the Dingo at 41cc. This little machine was purely a commuter vehicle and was an instant success, being low-priced and practical. Again a pressed frame was used, to keep the cost down, though by 1970 the engine size had increased to 49cc.

Although the V7 was developed on the back of a government enquiry for police and army motor cycles, the Falcone had long been a favourite with military and police users and it was felt that a development of that machine would almost certainly encourage more public authority sales. So the design team at Mandello went to work on creating the Nuovo Falcone, which was announced in 1971. The public displayed an interest in this big single, too, so it was offered to the market at large in various forms, but it never reached the volumes of sales needed to justify its continuance in the range beyond 1976.

Racing was used by Moto Guzzi as a means of testing the V7 to its limit. Raimondo Riva rode both Special and Sport versions with some success in production bike racing, while the Brambilla brothers Ernesto and Vittorio also 'had a go' with the Sport. (Vittorio later went on to race cars and became well known for his exploits aboard Formula One Alfa Romeos and his contribution to Alfa Romeo's World Sports Car Championship successes). Ernesto Brambilla, Raimondo Riva and

Luigi Agostini continued to race motor cycles and notched up a few successes on the way. Moto Guzzis took part in the 1972 Imola 200, the Bol D'Or 24 Hours, the Barcelona 24 Hours and the Spa 24 Hours.

At the same time, the big V-twin had been developed into a range of models under the guidance of Lino Tonti. The Sport was followed by the California and Ambassador models. The 750S followed the original 750 models, the principal modification being the introduction of dual disc brakes on the front wheel. Tonti also developed the Moto Guzzi frame to make it more durable and thoroughly manageable. Pride of place in the SEIMM era of Moto Guzzi's past, though, goes to the 850. This machine not only led to the next successful police machine, it also spawned the Le Mans – as truly beautiful a piece of motor cycle engineering as any around in its time.

By 1973 the SEIMM board decided that its job of recovering the fortunes of Moto Guzzi was virtually complete, so it was time to return the company to the private sector. The transfer came in a very different form from anything visualised by the traditional motor cycling fraternity, as the company passed into the hands of Alejandro de Tomaso, an Argentinian of Italian descent. De Tomaso had moved to Italy in 1955 to take up motor racing. He had proved to be an excellent driver and used that experience to establish himself on the car scene, setting up the de Tomaso company to make cars in Turin. Backed by Ford, he took over the Ghia plant and turned it into a Ford development centre, and then bought up the Vignale coachworks, which became the production centre for his new car, the Pantera. Ford adopted the Pantera as its own product in 1972 and de Tomaso used the money he gained from that project, together with some of his own fortune, to buy out the ailing Benelli company at Pesaro. He had decided that the Italian motor cycle had great potential and should be geared to taking on the Japanese competition.

The Japanese had already decimated the British motor cycle industry and Alejandro de Tomaso was determined that the same thing should not happen in Italy. So, when it became clear that Moto Guzzi was also on the market, he stepped in and made a bid. SEIMM felt his offer was entirely appropriate to the value of the company and believed that it would safeguard both the company's future and the jobs it provided. It was de Tomaso's view that the organisation and technology available in Italy could match what was available in Japan – all he had to do was develop those two aspects at Moto Guzzi and Benelli, with higher volumes of production minimising manufacturing costs.

The merging of Moto Guzzi and Benelli was, from a business point of view, entirely logical as a means of reconstructing Italy's motor cycle industry, but it was a step which provoked much scepticism at Mandello del Lario. There had been a great deal of disruption already at the factory, and now a 'foreigner' (as Guzzi workers and management saw him), with no experience of the industry, was to take over the firm. Many of the workers were anxious about job losses, and the merger with Benelli did little to inspire confidence, either, but de Tomaso made the new group into the largest motor cycle manufacturing concern in Europe.

By the 1970s the new version of the Stornello Scrambler was on the market. Not as pretty as the earlier version, it nevertheless was in tune with contemporary styling trends and fitted well into the market for lightweight scramblers, being within the 125cc class.

While the V7 was carving out new markets for Moto Guzzi, the company was still holding on to its traditional markets. The Mark 4 Trotter, with a fully cowled engine, filled the need for a junior moped. This one actually has pedals.

nally the V7 Special appeared at the 'big' end of the market. This is a 1970 example, finished in white. Many
7 Specials made their way into police service. But this machine also formed the basis of the machines that
ould bring Moto Guzzis back to the race track.

he 750cc class saw
oto Guzzi in more
ces as 1971 advanced
d this picture shows
aimondo Riva at the
rthe Circuit of Le
ans riding for his life,
partnership with
bbondio Sciaresa, in
e 1971 Bol d'Or, the
5th anniversary event.
eliability was improving
d the pair managed to
ish in sixth place. Of
urse, the biggest
mpetition came from
ologna in the form of
ucati, whose big
-twins were getting
er better.

This is Piazzalunga astride the V7 Sport at Monza in June 1971, where the machine made its debut in the Monza 500. Piazzalunga shared the ride with Raimondo Riva, and they finished in third place. Note that the front brake is still in a drum, though with two leading shoes it was pretty efficient. Even so, that front brake would come in for some attention before long.

The best result in 1971 came from a young man who was later to drive on four wheels for Alfa Romeo with notable success. Vittorio Brambilla is seen here in typical style, riding his V7 Sport to the limit in the Vallelunga 500 Kilometre Race, in which he finished second.

The Furghino was the latest development in Dingo-powered goods carriers. This is one of the last examples, produced in 1971. The Furghino was the Dingotre's replacement and used shaft-drive instead of chain. Like the Aiace before it, this little machine boasted a doorless cab, and like the Dingotre was exempt from road licensing. Its driver didn't even need to hold a driving licence. Its demise left a gap in the market, but Moto Guzzi needed the workshop floor-space.

Having inspired a revival of interest in large motor cycles, Moto Guzzi was faced with a renewed interest in big singles and so the Nuovo Falcone was introduced to fill that gap. Styled in the mould of the smaller Guzzi machines, it had a red frame and white fuel tank, mudguards and side panels. This is an early 1972 example.

The growth of sporting interest around the V7 encouraged Moto Guzzi to develop the Special into the V7 Sport in 1971. Distinguished by its scarlet frame and light olive green metallic fuel tank, it was still fitted with drum brakes. The two leading shoe design gave very good stopping power, though fashion would soon dictate that Guzzi, like many other motor cycle makers, should fit disc front brakes.

Testing the V7 Sport at Monza during April, before the Imola 200 race, Vittorio Brambilla (*Inset, left*) decided that the four leading shoe brakes really weren't adequate for the kind of ride he was expecting. Brambilla was a true racer and he went to Imola with every intention of winning, so disc brakes were to be an essential part of the V7 Sport Corsa. Three V7 Sports were entered for the Imola race on 23 April 1972, with Australian Jack Findlay riding alongside Vittorio Brambilla and Guido Mandracci. All three machines were fitted with triple disc brakes – one each side of the front wheel and a single disc on the back wheel, the drive shaft occupying the other side of the wheel. After a hard race, Brambilla was the first of three to finish, coming into eighth place. Two places behind him came Findlay in tenth, with Mandracci right behind him in eleventh. (*Main picture*): Guido Mandracci astride his V7 at Imola. He is working pretty hard in this view, as the whole Guzzi team did to hang on to the string of Ducatis ahead of them.

The 90-degree V-twin engine of the V7 Sport was an 82.5mm x 70mm unit, giving 748cc displacement. The heavily ribbed crankcase was a feature of the Sport power unit, as was the dual ignition. The roadgoing version was now fitted with an alternator and the clutch was a two-plate dry unit. The power output was 52bhp and it dragged the production V7 Sport along at 125mph.

Having established a reputation for performance and reliability with the original V7, in 1972 Moto Guzzi announced the V850. America was a key target market and this is the Eldorado 850, a big, beefy machine that didn't quite have the look of a Harley Davidson, but it certainly had the performance, the reliability and the comfort.

By 1974 the 850GT was in the Guzzi portfolio. This machine bore no resemblance whatever to the GT of many years before but it really was a Grand Tourer in every sense. Despite being 100cc bigger than the V7 sport, it produced one brake horsepower less. But it was a gutsy, torquey engine that seemed as though it would run forever – and many of them are still running!

CHAPTER ELEVEN

INTO THE DE TOMASO ERA

The Junior market was still very important to Moto Guzzi. After all, if you captured the loyalty of youngsters before they needed a driving licence and before their machine needed registration, then you stood a chance of keeping their custom for ever. So the 'tiddlers' continued to be offered and sold. Here's the very neat Cross 50 of 1975. Looking wholly the part of a motocross machine, some were actually run in such events.

While Alejandro de Tomaso's takeover of Moto Guzzi was initially greeted with apprehension, it was inevitable and ultimately was seen as having been for the good of the company and the people who worked there. Of course, some jobs were lost and there was a period of 'badge engineering' when de Tomaso, who didn't like big twins, decided that the way to beat the Japanese invasion was to meet them head-on. This meant using multi-cylinder engines, and Benelli had a number of designs in their portfolio.

It was essential, in de Tomaso's view, to reduce the cost of manufacturing the V-Twin if it was to survive at all, and so the specification had to be reduced. This involved replacing the timing gears in the engine with chains and sprockets and using common parts between models. The 750S3 was the last of the line, for in 1975 a new sporting model was to appear. Despite Alejandro de Tomaso's dislike of big twin-engined bikes, the new model was to become probably the most successful production sporting motor cycle of its era. The 850 Le Mans was a well-balanced machine with excellent handling characteristics and the power and torque to make it a thoroughly sporty ride, while still being tractable enough to be a very attractive touring machine. Styling of the Le Mans was absolutely up-to-date, with lines and angles well coordinated to make it a very pretty machine, whether static or on the move.

Within a very short space of time from de Tomaso's takeover, two transverse-engined overhead cam four-cylinder machines were designed and built. The first was a 500, offered for sale under the Benelli badge, while the second was a smaller 350 machine, badged as a Moto Guzzi. These were to be Italy's main challenge to the multi-cylindered Japanese onslaught. For a time, they were successful. Along with this new Guzzi 350, a Guzzi 250 twin was also launched. It was a parallel twin, designed at Pesaro, and so was essentially a rebadged Benelli. It was also made at Pesaro, which didn't please everybody at Mandello del Lario, though there was little they could do about it. One other small Benelli which became a Guzzi in that same period was the 125cc single-cylinder model, offered in two forms as the Turismo and the Tutteterrano ('All Terrain') models.

Two new 50cc machines were also launched soon after the de Tomaso takeover. These were the Cross, named to imply an ability to ride off road, and the Nibbio, a motor cycle-styled moped aimed at roadgoing youngsters who wanted something that looked the part, even if it was legally restricted to 40km/h (legally defined mopeds of up to 50cc engine displacement could be used on the road without registration plates as long as they were not able to be ridden at speeds greater than 40km/h). Accompanying these two miniatures was another lightweight, aimed this time mainly at the lady commuter. This was the Chiu, powered by a 50cc engine. Looking very much like the Trotter, it had a front-mounted basket to provide space for limited shopping.

In the wake of the Benelli 500 and the Moto Guzzi 350 four-cylinder models, Mandello del Lario came up in 1974 with a pair of single overhead camshaft transverse fours, to be known as the 350GTS and the 400GTS. Again aimed at taking on the Japanese invaders, these were blatantly styled in the same manner as the Japanese machines, while retaining just enough Italian flavour to identify their homeland. Using a one-piece crankshaft and central chain drive for the camshaft, their design was clearly influenced by production economics, but these fours were certainly up to the job and made some contribution to Moto Guzzi's fortunes. The 350 produced 31bhp while the 400 turned in 40bhp. Top speeds were just under and just over 100mph respectively and the 400GTS had a front disc brake in place of the drum of the smaller model.

Perhaps one of the most important Moto Guzzi models to emerge from the Guzzi–Benelli tie-up was the 254, a 231cc four-cylinder model. The first lightweight four-cylinder machine to be manufactured in quantity, its title was derived from its nominal 250cc capacity and its four cylinders. Its styling and mechanical design were revolutionary and it caused quite a stir when it was launched in 1975 at the Milan Motor Cycle Show. With its cast alloy wheels, front disc brake and integrally designed fuel-tank/rider's seat/rear mudguard, it looked thoroughly well designed and it was certainly well built. However, it did not seem to capture the imagination of the public and sales were poor, so by 1981 it was gone from the range. Its lack of success may be partly explained by the fact that the same machine was also offered as the Benelli Four, and the resentment of badge engineering was too strong for the 254 to be accepted as a true Moto Guzzi.

A gap was perceived in the Guzzi line-up between the entry level scooter/moped models and the 250. The company hoped to fill this gap by taking the cycle parts of the 254 and installing into the frame a new single overhead camshaft parallel twin. The 125cc power unit with its twin carburettors produced 16bhp, sufficient to reach 130km/h, though it certainly needed its five-speed gearbox. Like the 254, this new 125-2C4T was equipped with electric starting and the same integrated design bodywork, though it was more brightly coloured to fit market demand.

While these multi-cylinder and entry level developments were taking place, the design team at Mandello del Lario remained keen to preserve the V-twin. Lino Tonti had already produced designs for a 350 and a 500, and in 1977 the V50, a 490cc variation on the Carcano-designed original, was to be launched, along with the V35, a 350cc alternative. These engines were ultimately to be stretched to 750cc, replacing the original 750 from Giulio Carcano's drawing-board, though that engine was in turn ultimately stretched to as much as 1100cc. The V50 and the V35 found themselves Americanised at the end of 1981, though the introduction of the V50 Monza brought back the European style to Moto Guzzis.

These V-engined motor cycles are the very essence of Moto Guzzi and ultimately, despite his very long tenure of office, Alejandro de Tomaso was unable to shift the public's perception of what makes a good modern Moto Guzzi. By 1993 de Tomaso was in poor health and his company was beginning to struggle, so a company called TIM (Temporary Integrated Management), a subsidiary of Finprogetti SpA (a small and privately owned Italian merchant bank) was appointed to take over the running of Moto Guzzi, although de Tomaso remained President. With the demise of the Benelli name, manufacturing was again focused on Mandello del Lario, and the company was to be reorganised once more.

Alongside the Cross came the Nibbio. Both the Nibbio and the Cross featured a 50cc engine/five-speed gearbox power train originally developed by Benelli, for this was the de Tomaso era of Moto Guzzi and Benelli had been brought in to contribute. These two little machines were launched in 1973 at the Milan Show and continued in production until 1982. Pretty and functional, they sold well.

Back to big Guzzis, here's the very tidy 750S of 1974/5, now featuring dual hydraulic disc front brakes and a number of other detail changes from the V7 Sport. For example, the engine and gearbox were mildly modified and the exhaust was now fitted with this large silencer-inclusive black tailpipe. The stylised eagle motif appeared for the first time on the side panel, while the single dual seat and the paint colours were all new.

The 850, a big touring machine, set the pattern for a line of Moto Guzzi tourers which became more and more American in style. This 1974/5 example has the crash bars, the pillion grab-bar, the Harley-style silencers and the chrome strips that characterised that style. The single front disc and rear drum brakes would soon give way to multiple discs.

In 1974 a new two-cylinder two-stroke with five-speed gearbox, one of the first products of the 'de Tomaso' era, went on sale, having been announced to the market in the spring of 1973. It was a parallel twin, the first Moto Guzzi derivative of a Benelli original, and it was a sporty bike for young riders who wanted to get on to the first rung of the ladder to real motor-cycling. This is an early model with drum brakes, but these were replaced by hydraulic discs by 1975.

A pair of 125 singles were the next offering from the Benelli–Guzzi link-up. Both had five-speed gearboxes ar were tidy little machines. This one, the 125 Turismo, was the popular road model, with a top speed of a little ov 50mph. The utility sector of the market bought these motor cycles in some numbers, as did the youth market.

Partnering the 125TS was the 'Tutteterrano', the all-terrain version of the 125. The two machines shared completely common frame, though they looked very different when built. This model was not intended f motocross but rather for trail riding, and it certainly looked the part. This version had a drum front brake inste of the disc of the Turismo. Both models sold well, but were pensioned off in 1981.

Triple disc brakes are an instantly recognisable feature of the 1975 V1000 I Convert. This was Moto Guzzi's most prestigious motor cycle yet, with a 948cc engine, two-speed automatic torque converter transmission (hence the name 'Convert'), dual side crash bars, metallic paint, rider's screen and all the other accessories that make a big luxurious touring bike. It was, of course, a success. Originally intended for police use, it was on the general market for ten years.

The 50cc market continued to have a Moto Guzzi in its ranks well into the 1970s. This is the Dingo MM, last of the Dingo line, which was fitted with an automatic centrifugal clutch and pedals – no gearbox. Once again, it served the shopper/commuter/youth markets well.

Last in the long line of commuter/shopper mopeds was the Chiu. With its shopping basket on the front, it was clear where this 40cc machine was aimed. The successor to the Trotter, and using the same concept of pressed steel frame and integral fuel tank, the Chiu used a 50cc engine, a single-speed transmission and a centrifugal automatic clutch, just like the Dingo MM.

Inspired by Japanese technology, but not copied from that source, the 350GTS was launched in the 1974 model year and shared its power unit with a Benelli (hardly surprisingly, since Alejandro de Tomaso had merged the two companies). The unitary engine/gearbox assembly was the first Guzzi to be transversely mounted. The four exhaust pipes ran into two, then split again into four silencers. This was a Japanese trend that Moto Guzzi could have done without, but the 350GTS was a fine, near 100mph, machine. Within a year the front drum brake was replaced with a 300mm disc.

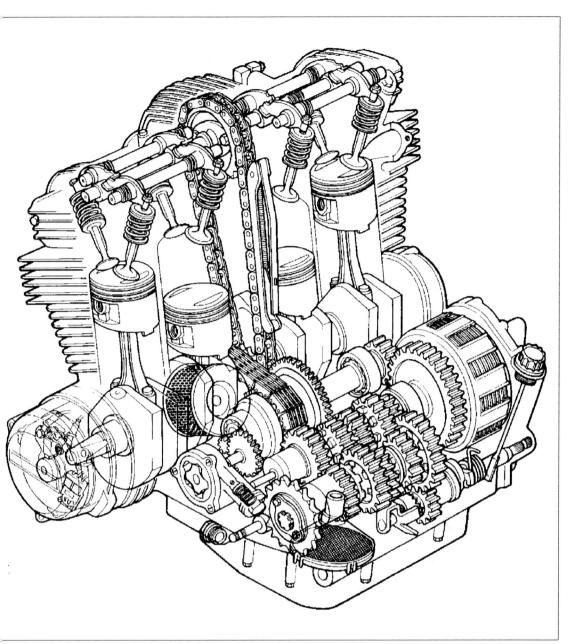

ere's the transverse engine/gearbox assembly of the 350GTS. With a bore and stroke of 50mm x 44mm, the ersquare engine could rev up to near 10,000rpm, yielding peak power of 31bhp at 9,200rpm. Note the timing ain running up the middle of the engine to the single overhead camshaft and the very neat, typically Moto izzi, five-speed gearbox.

Mini motor bikes (sometimes called 'Monkey Bikes') were highly fashionable in the 1970s and grand prix mot[e]
racing did a lot to promote them – this was a far cry from the original concept of a parachutable machine f[e]
military use. The Moto Guzzi Magnum 50 was an extension of that concept, with its Dingo-based 50cc engir[e]
and five-speed gearbox. The five-spoke alloy wheels with balloon tyres delivered a very comfortable ride, but it w[a]
not really a street bike.

The 254 was another styling breakthrough for Moto Guzzi. Another transverse four-cylinder-engined machine,
was not quite a scaled-down version of the 350/400SS. The engine looked different and the frame, which hous[e]
a normal-style fuel tank, was a simple tubular cradle. The bodywork, however, was revolutionary in that the ta[r]
cowling, side panels and seat moulding were all made of thermoplastic material and were keyed together, so bei[n]
easy to remove yet conveying the impression of a single top 'dressing'. The five-spoke alloy wheels were new, [.]
was the instrument cluster in the top of the tank panel. There was also a Benelli variant, known as the 'Quattro[.]

In similar style was the 125 2c 4T. This was quite literally, mechanically at least, half of a 254. The cycle parts, panelling, instruments and wheels were all 'borrowed' from the 254. The two-cylinder engine was of 124cc displacement, though the instruments were elevated back to the handlebars. It was a sporty little bike, but was only on offer for a couple of years between 1979 and 1981.

Back on the big scene, the 850T3 Polizia found its way into the motor-cycling arena. The big 850 Grand Tourer was enlisted into the Polizia Stradale and fitted with the full police kit. A big machine, the 850T3 could easily cope with the extra weight, but of course, the extra mass needed greater stopping power, so triple disc brakes (two in front and one behind) gave it that controllability.

Now here's a real 'leading edge' machine. Take one 850 engine, the basic V7 design concept and bring them together into a 'tweaked' combination, lighter and aerodynamically cleaner than the tourers and what do you have? The 850 Le Mans. First in a long line of big 'cafe racers', the Le Mans was also the first Guzzi to feature perforated brake discs, aimed at keeping them cool under hard application. This is a 1978 example of the Le Mans.

In April 1978 the 1000SP was adopted for police and military use and this publicity shot shows twenty of the sitting in front of the Guzzi wind tunnel. The original caption read 'Nate nell galleria del vento' ('Born out of wind tunnel').

no Tonti's revamp of Giulio Carcano's original V7 big twin brought smaller engines to the market, as well as rge ones. The decision to replace the 350/400SS models resulted in the V35, created in 1977. A well-balanced in with shaft drive and disc brakes, it was a sub-100mph machine, but was sold against the changes in Italian hicle taxation legislation. The 350 class had been ignored by Italian motor cycle makers for too long, but the zzi V35 was to change that.

he early 1980s brought the 850T4, which borrowed the 1000SP's 'bikini' fairing (so-named because it covered ly the 'top' of the motor cycle). In all other aspects, the T4 looked much the same as the T3, though in practice e engine was now fitted with Nigusil bores, the carburettors were different, the gearbox was now five-speed and few minor cosmetic changes were made.

Deciding that a sporty version of the V35 was called for, Moto Guzzi introduced the V35 Imola. Looking remarkably like the 254, it was actually not a direct 'crib' of the smaller machine but it did convey a sense of family style. This was a true 100mph machine and was notable for the reappearance of the eagle motif on the fuel tanks of Moto Guzzi motor cycles. This machine didn't have the performance of the bigger Le Mans, but it did offer a sporty bike for the heavily taxed Italian market.

The American-style motor cycle was now firmly established as a part of the Moto Guzzi range and in 1982 the California II appeared, powered by a 950cc engine. The application of chrome and paint on the mudguards and the general appearance of the machine certainly made it an attractive bike, but ironically more examples were actually sold in Europe than in America!

Harking back to the styling of the Moto Guzzi Le Mans model of 1978, the V65 was introduced in 1981/2 to bridge the gap that was appearing in the market between 350s and the ever-enlarging big machines that had now reached 1000cc. The V650SP was the answer, finished in gold, blue or red. Looking like a hybrid between the earlier 1000SP and the Le Mans, it stayed in the catalogue until 1987.

Moto Cross became increasingly popular as the 1980s moved on, so Moto Guzzi brought this little machine to the market. The 125TT (Tutteterrano – All-Terrain) was powered by a liquid-cooled 125cc single (the half-254 was abandoned as too expensive to manufacture). A de Tomaso-inspired Guzzi/Benelli product, the 125TT didn't actually make it into production until 1985. It was very popular in the important youth market.

When the TT was launched in 1985, it was decided that a small American-style bike would sell quite well, too, out came the 125 Custom. It had the same frame and mechanics as the TT, but different bodywork. It also had screen, American-style, and a hefty low exhaust. Alloy wheels completed the specification of this youth cruise which again was sold in Guzzi and Benelli versions.

The 850T5 brought minimal aerodynamics to the big tourer, along with a number of subtle changes. Th cylinder heads now had more squared cam covers, the pillion passenger's grab-rail was of square section and th front fairing was also more angular (and positively ugly). The wheels were now five-spoke, though they bore strong resemblance to the T4's seven spokes.

In 1983 the sales team at Moto Guzi thought it was time for a Tutteterrano 350 and so a year later this very functional-looking V35TT appeared. The 18in rear and 21in front wheels aided the appearance of this enduro machine, which also featured the more squared cam covers. Electric starting was not yet common to enduro bikes, but this Guzzi had it.

The first 1000cc Le Mans model was announced in 1984. Following the contemporary styling of the V50 Monza I, it had the softer line of motor cycles of the time. It looked a handsome bike, but it failed to satisfy its markets. Quality and reliability were below standard and exhaust emissions were little different from earlier models; with countries becoming ever more critical, sales fell far short of target.

Back in the world of the V35, the continuing trend towards American cruisers took another step at Mandello del Lario when the V35 Florida entered the range in 1986. With hard side panniers and shaped dual seats, as well as the tall screen, this was the perfect poser's bike for those whose wallets wouldn' stretch to the Californi Realistically, though, if you didn't need big bike performance, it was a fine 350 cruiser.

An all-black engine/driveline installation characterised the next enduro in the Guzzi range, the 650 NTX. (I could be said that the current enduro-style Guzzi, the Quota, has its origins in this machine.) The same style wa applied to a 350 NTX, which followed the 'African' fashion, set by the machines built to compete in events like th Paris–Dakar Rally. It was another case of Guzzi trying to be all things to all men.

After the fairly disastrous experience of the Le Mans 1000 (also known as the Le Mans IV), Moto Guzzi tried to make amends with the introduction of the revised Le Mans 1000 (generally known as the Le Mans V, though not so labelled). The fuller fairing was still not an all-enveloping fairing in the style of contemporary Japanese machines, largely because the big V-twin was very difficult to hide inside a fairing that didn't look ridiculously wide.

Mille GT was the name given in 1987 to the minimal specification ('standard') 1000cc Moto Guzzi. With wire wheels and no excessive bodywork, it had something of the highly successful 850T about it. It also responded to the German market need for a standard 'no frills' machine by providing a 1000cc alternative to the higher performance Le Mans or the big cruisers.

Slightly down-sized from the big brawny Moto Guzzis, the 650 GT (labelled in Italy as the Sessantacinque GT) was a compact grand tourer from the V65 family, introduced in 1987 and aimed at the home market in Italy. Again, road taxation was the motive for producing a smaller machine for domestic sale. It was actually a physically smaller machine, too. It was not a sparkling performer, some testers feeling that it lacked something from the earlier V65, but it did the job.

Moto Guzzi did try one fully faired design in late 1987. The V35 Falco had a quad cam engine with four valves per cylinder in an all-black finished engine/gearbox assembly. The aerodynamics helped it to 110+ mph, according to claims, though it could well have been capable of more. Had it not been for the continuing fall in 350cc sales, this machine might have found its way into production, but sadly it didn't.

The Quota is a real enduro bike. The 1989 Quota 1000 has minimal bodywork, high seating and high ground clearance. With a substantial underpan to protect the bottom front corner of the frame and the engine's sump, this was a real trail bike, truly capable of being ridden in the rough. Clearly aimed at the BMW enduro market, this Guzzi became very popular for its ruggedness.

No fairings, no body bits, just a raw motor cycle – this out-and-out sports bike was the 1000S of 1989, a bike that recalled the 750S of fifteen years before. It was a big hairy beast, fitted with the 82bhp 1000 engine and a five-speed gearbox. With a maximum road speed of 144mph, this machine was quite a handful and it was a perfect café racer.

In 1990 the 125 BX came on sale, powered by the water-cooled single of the TT model. Basically it was a 125TT brought up to date, with disc brakes at front and rear. Plastic mudguards and body fittings were now commonplace on all motor cycles of this type, so Moto Guzzi was in tune with the rest of the market.

This handsome cruiser is the 1990 Nevada 750. Carrying soft rear panniers, Harley Electraglide fashion, the Nevada was not a big seller in the United States, but it was popular among cruiser-enthusiasts all across Europe. With its wire wheels, Easy Rider handlebars and low, comfortable seating position, it represented excellent value for money. In 350 form, it was the ideal entry level machine.

The other 750 for 1990 was the SP, a Eurostyle tourer with fine lines and excellent market appeal. Launched to take on the BMW and Japanese tourers in the same size category, it was a very clean machine, with a half fairing and a smooth body line. The 750 was a popular machine, but when pitted against competition from the likes of Ducati it lost out in performance and handling.

This is probably Moto Guzzi's most exciting racing machine since the Quattrovalvole or the Bicilindrica. The magnificent 1000cc Daytona racer was developed by former dentist Dr John Wittner, and this example sits in the entrance to Moto Guzzi's museum at Mandello del Lario. The Wittner racer began life in 1987, winning the Pro-twins championship that year, and going on to be adopted as a production model by 1990.

Launched in 1989, the prototype Daytona 1000 was first released to the press and planned for production a year later. However, it was to be a couple of years before the Daytona took to the road in the hands of new owners. Handling and performance were promised to be outstanding, with a catalogued 150mph top speed.

This is what the Daytona production model was planned to look like. This one carries Dr John's autograph. The production version differed slightly, but it was a pretty exciting motor cycle, however you looked at it. Interestingly, the engine design came from the drawing-board of a man first associated with Moto Guzzi almost sixty years before – Umberto Todero.

CHAPTER TWELVE

TOWARDS A NEW MILLENNIUM

While the Daytona was struggling into production, the latest version of the California, the Anniversario, was taking to the streets. A leaner and cleaner machine than its immediate predecessor, the Anniversario was created to mark the 70th anniversary of Moto Guzzi (a year late, but none the less, the event was marked). Each machine in this series carried an engraved plate and was delivered with a certificate signed by Alejandro de Tomaso. The saddle on these machines was genuine leather.

For almost twenty years Moto Guzzi was under the ownership of the De Tomaso empire, in the form of De Tomaso Industries and later Trident Rowan Industries. Alejandro De Tomaso had married the American heiress Elizabeth Haskell, and much of her wealth had gone to support her husband's not inconsiderable fortune in the expansion of their corporate empire. Her family's business was Rowan Controller Group, and her brother Amory was chairman. The ultimate integration of the various business entities resulted in the creation of Trident Rowan Group Incorporated.

While Alejandro De Tomaso was always opposed to big-twins, it is perhaps ironic that the key to Moto Guzzi's true success in modern times was the big V-twin, ranging from 350cc to 1100cc machines. The mopeds and lightweights were now to disappear and the whole focus of manufacturing concentrated on the various V-engined models. This came about in no small part because of the appointment of TIM (Temporary Integrated Management) by Finprogetti. In 1993–4 Arnolfo Sacchi, now chief executive, headed a viability study which determined, much to the relief of employees and suppliers, that the company should continue in business.

The year 1995 saw Sacchi's work rewarded. The company recorded a profit and production rose to 5,300. In August 1996 Alejandro de Tomaso resigned as president of the group and De Tomaso Industries was reorganised as Trident Rowan Group Incorporated. Paid up capital in Moto Guzzi had been increased from 2 billion to 5 billion lire in January 1996 and in the late summer of that year Mario Tozzi-Condivi became president of Moto Guzzi. By the year's end the company's production had grown to over 6,000 units and turnover was up to 76 billion lire. The company was now back into profit and so, at the beginning of 1997, a further increase in paid up capital was announced, bringing it now to 12 billion lire, by means of TRGI privately placing 6 billion US dollars worth of shares on the NASDAQ stock market in New York.

In May 1997 Finprogetti sold its majority shareholding to the Tamarix Corporation, an American merchant banking group, which now took control of Moto Guzzi. Oscar Cecchinato succeeded Arnolfo Sacchi as chief executive and was bent on expanding the company and its production to new levels. In the financial plan announced by Cecchinato, Tamarix had allocated 55 billion lire to the development of Moto Guzzi: 30 billion for product development, 13 billion for new plant and machinery, and the remaining 12 billion for logistics and building work. By the end of that year share capital had been further increased to 25 billion lire. A further 9 billion lire had been added to turnover for the year and production was increased again, now to 6,300.

A series of events in the 1980s had a profound effect on the public image of Moto Guzzi and thus, indirectly, on the company's future. At this time the factory had no official racing programme but an American dentist, Dr John Wittner, keen to participate in endurance racing, launched his own race programme with a modified Guzzi Le Mans. After gaining support from Moto Guzzi North America and the US Moto Guzzi Club, Wittner approached the factory for development support to help him produce a spine-framed machine dedicated to racing. A modified two-valve Le Mans 992cc engine was fitted to the new frame and this machine went on to win the 1987 Pro-Twins, ridden by Doug Brauneck. By the end of the year that machine was producing 118bhp.

Umberto Todero produced an overhead cam four-valve engine for 'Dr John', with the intention of improving performance. However, this did not immediately achieve its goal and the 1988 season was not the success that 1987 had been. In Europe the battle of the twins contest led Moto Guzzi to build a few replicas of the 1987 Dr John machine for sale to the racing public. Wittner continued development work on his machine, but 1989 failed to repeat the success of 1987 either. At the end of the year he decided to quit racing and work with Moto Guzzi at Mandello del Lario to develop the production Daytona model. But Wittner's efforts had given Moto Guzzi a new focus, at least for a while, and the publicity had certainly been beneficial.

The production Daytona model was announced in 1989 but it was two years before it was manufactured in quantity, by which time many buyers had gone over to the competition. However, Moto Guzzi still enjoyed the lion's share of 'Ameri-cruisers' in Europe (not in the US, though), with the California in the large capacity class and the Nevada offered in 750 and 350 engine sizes. In developed form these two models continued to flourish into the twenty-first century. The Daytona continued in production until 1997, while the V10 Centauro appeared in 1998. Another exciting model was the Quota, an Enduro-type machine with a low seating position and lots of power.

Planned for 1998 was the exciting Ippogrifo, a touring 750 carrying the V7 model number. New for this model was the single rear damper, positioned under the rider's seat and connected from the frame to the progressive deformable quadrilateral rear suspension. The engine was developed from the aero version of the Guzzi engine, connected to a six-speed gearbox, and shaft-drive to the rear wheel was retained. For various reasons, mostly commercial, the 'Winged Horse' – Ippogrifo – never went beyond the development stage.

During that same year, 1998, plans were set in train to buy a new factory, a former Philips Electronics site, at Monza, with the intention of moving Moto Guzzi's manufacturing activity from Mandello del Lario, but leaving behind parts and service activities. However, several board members expressed serious concern and the workers were extremely reluctant to relocate, and so Oscar Cecchinato was replaced and the move to Monza cancelled. Dino Falciola stepped into the breach and succeeded in extricating Moto Guzzi from the deal with Philips, though the cancellation of the move jeopardised a deal Moto Guzzi was about to embark upon with Piaggio for a new 600cc single-cylinder engine and a 125cc scooter.

Today Moto Guzzi continues to nestle in the shadow of Mount Grigna and its loyal 360-strong workforce continues to manufacture motor cycles there. Under the leadership of Mario Scandellari, whose experience embraced senior management positions in Cagiva and Ducati, the company was to take a new direction. Most of the market for new machinery in the private sector is drawn from 'born again' motor-cyclists, and Moto Guzzi has to target the young and entry level markets again in order to achieve greater expansion. But whatever the uncertainties in management, the name Moto Guzzi will live on for a long time yet . . .

The Daytona 1000 finally made it into production. Potentially the most powerful Moto Guzzi ever, this 150mp demon was pretty sparse-looking by comparison with the 'superbikes' of other manufacturers but it was genuine superfast motor cycle. Note the transverse primary expansion box on this 1993 example. All in all, th Daytona was a very tight package.

Here's the Daytona's power house – the magnificent quad cam, four-valve, 1000cc engine. Exposed is the valve gear of one cylinder, so you can see the camshafts and exhaust valves. Also note the dual notched tooth belt camshaft drive. Apart from being quieter in operation, belt drive t the camshafts was more efficient than chains and belts are easier to replace. Astonishingly, this engine could deliver 130bhp in its highest state of tune.

In 1993 Moto Guzzi pulled off a true marketing coup. The newest engine in the range was a two-valve 1100, developed in collaboration with Dr John Wittner and Crane Engineering in Florida. It produced 90bhp in finished form and was much less complicated than the Daytona engine. Installed into a Daytona chassis with slightly revised bodywork, the result was a successor to the Le Mans, the 1100 Sport, which instantly outsold the Daytona model, being less expensive and less complicated but of very similar performance.

Strada Mille (Street 1000) was the name given to this machine, ultimately a successor to the SPIII. Wire-wheeled and with touring handlebars, this was a regular road machine which used the standard 1000 engine and the SP frame. Introduced in 1993, it was the last 'standard' 1000cc Moto Guzzi, and it was thought by some to be obsolescent when it was introduced. But it was a good reliable motor cycle for the rider who wanted an uncomplicated Guzzi.

By the mid-1990s cruisers provided the entry level Guzzi in the form of the 350 Nevada NT. A no-frills Easy Rider, the 350 version clearly didn't give a sparkling performance, but it was the least expensive route to a big V-twin Moto Guzzi. If you wanted to spend a little more, then the 750 Nevada looked exactly the same, but had the advantage of the bigger engine.

If the bigger Nevada still didn't fill your needs then the California 1100IE, with fuel injection engine, certainly ought to do the trick. This is the ultimate Moto Guzzi cruiser, so much so that BMW decided to break into the cruiser market, but they came nowhere near matching this big Italian, which even outperformed the 1340 Harley Davidson Dyna Glide.

y 1997 the flagship of
e Moto Guzzi line-up was
e V10 Centauro, a
00cc Grand Tourer. This
as an unashamed
tempt to combine retro
ith the latest technology,
t maintaining a modern
e. Technically it worked
d the resulting machine
as a four-valve-engined
otor cycle with much of
e Daytona's performance
otential but the more
mfortable, relaxed riding
osition of the tourer.

The Ippogrifo was another mythical beast, this one half-horse, half-eagle. The Moto Guzzi of that name was to be a 750cc 'retro' tourer in the spirit of the British Triumph Bonneville. Announced in 1996, it was to be a high rider with a mono-shock rear suspension and wire wheels, and was to be powered by Umberto Todero's Guzzi aero engine, modified for road use. But reorganisation and corporate manoeuvres caused it to be sidelined.

The most uncompromising sporting Moto Guzzi of the late 1990s was the Daytona RS, a four-valve raceable sportster of 150mph potential. It was probably the best Moto Guzzi ever built in terms of the technology of its design and manufacture and its handling was superb. But the sales success of the 1100 Sport overshadowed it, so the Daytona never sold in the numbers it might have. Doubtless in time it will become a much sought-after classic.

The Sport 1100 was indistinguishable from the Daytona RS, except for two-things – the name on the rear seat fairing and the tell-tale cambox on the engine, letting everybody know it was a two-valve engine and therefore an 1100 Sport, not a Daytona. For a worthwhile saving on price, the Sport forfeited only a little in performance to its sibling and, being the same chassis, it had the same handling characteristics.

Key models in the 1998 line-up at Moto Guzzi were the Nevada, the California, the Centauro, the Daytona Sport and the 1100 Sport. All these models are on display at Mandello del Lario in the reception area – it is an impressive sight.

Approaching the new millennium, Moto Guzzi still has a classic range of motor cycles, beginning with the Nevada Club, which is available in 350cc and 750cc versions. Here's the 750 variant, a relatively uncluttered design for a cruiser, still with wire wheels and now sporting a two-tone fuel tank with top and bottom halves in different colours, rather than the colour panel insert as previously used. This distinguished the Nevada from the California at a distance. Today, the Nevada is the 350NT and there is a police version available, too, the 350NT PA.

There were several versions of the California – the Special, the Evoluzione and the EV, as well as police variations. This is the 1100 California Evolution, with just about everything in sight chrome-plated. Despite its size and weight, the California is still a high performance machine, with a 125mph top speed.

The Centauro comes in four variations now. This is the GT, with its touring screen and high position rear-view mirrors. Still a snappy looker despite having been on the market for over five years, the Centauro GT is also still a performer, with the quad cam four-valve engine and a five-speed gearbox.

Also in the Centauro GT range is the V10 GT Sport, finished, appropriately, in red. With a short top fairing and an air scoop fairing running under the engine's sump, this looks like an out-and-out sportster, except perhaps for the high mirrors. Another hallmark of the Centauro Sport are the white stripes that run over the tank and down to the outer edges of the saddle. The Centauro Sport looked very similar, except that it didn't have the high mounted mirrors and also came in green.

The best roadgoing enduro from Moto Guzzi was the Quota 1100ES, a big hairy motor cycle that not only looked the part, but also did the job. With the two-valve engine coupled to a five-speed gearbox, it produced just under 120mph top road speed with handling to match. One significant improvement over the earlier Quota was the much lower seating position at 32.25in, which made it accessible to very tall riders.

The 1100 Sport Corsa became the most refined two-valve sports machine on offer from Mandello del Lario b 1998. Several minor refinements made this the most exciting motor cycle yet. Fitted with Carillo connecting rod on the inside and Termignoni carbon fibre exhaust on the outside, it was capable of over 150mph.

Hoping to recapture the spirit of the V7 Sport of the early 1970s, Moto Guzzi's newest machine is the V11 Sport It was first announced in 1997 but took two years to reach production. The latest form of the 1100 two-valve engine produced 91bhp and was coupled to a six-speed gearbox by means of a two dry plate clutch. A littl slower than the Daytona and 1100 Sport Corsa, it could still turn in 137.5mph. The flagship of Mandello de Lario, this motor cycle will take the financially stronger company into the next century with pride.

MOTO GUZZIS ON FOUR WHEELS

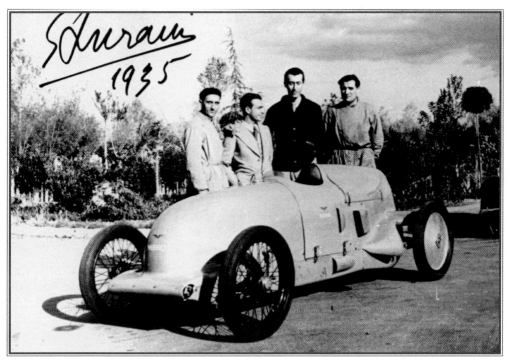

Count Giovanni ('Johnny') Lurani's 1935 'Nibbio' 500cc record-breaker.

Carlo Guzzi's ambition had always been to design and manufacture the world's finest motor cycles, and his innovative skills and qualitative approach to manufacturing helped him to achieve those twin goals. And it was those very characteristics that attracted a number of small car builders to his products. The tremendous reputation acquired by Moto Guzzi engines for near unburstable reliability prompted a number of would-be record breakers to take a close look at Guzzi engines when they were planning to run for sub-1-litre speed and endurance records.

Aiming to set a 500cc record on four wheels in 1935 was Count Giovanni Lurani, already a well-known racing driver, approached Moto Guzzi to supply the power unit for his new venture. He chose a wide-angled V-twin 500cc engine and it was duly installed into a little streamlined four-wheeler named Nibbio. 'Johnny' Lurani was about to go record breaking, aided by Ulisse Guzzi, Carlo's son.

The 500cc Bicilindrica engine was fine-tuned in Guzzi's workshops to develop 50bhp. This tremendous power output compared favourably with many sporting small cars of the time which had engines of twice the displacement (for example, the Riley Nine was among the most successful 1100cc cars of the time and the Brooklands and Imp Riley models were producing little more than 50bhp in race trim on four cylinders). Lurani and Guzzi went off to the Firenze–Mare road on 5 November 1935 and Nibbio duly set new speed records for the Standing and Flying Kilometre and One Mile distances in the Under-500cc Class. In May 1939 Count Lurani took the little car to Berlin and on the Berlin–Munich Autobahn set new records, reaching a speed of 108mph.

Some time after the Second World War Piero Taruffi, a racing motor-cyclist and racing driver of considerable talent, decided to have go at 500cc record breaking. His machine, the Bisiluro, was most unusual in that it was a 'catamaran on wheels' – two cylindrical-shaped bodies, each on two wheels, linked together. The driver sat on the left-hand portion. This machine was designed and built by Taruffi himself. Not having the same level of factory support as Count Lurani had enjoyed, Taruffi's engine could not match the power output of the Lurani machine, though he still managed to squeeze 129mph from his machine in 1948, setting several new 500 records on the way.

In 1955 'Johnny' Lurani returned to sub-half-litre record breaking and built a new car for the purpose. This was Nibbio II, which was to be powered by a 350cc

Piero Taruffi's 'Bisiluro'.

single Moto Guzzi engine. This car went to Monza's Autodrome and set a whole string of new middle- and long-distance records between 1956 and 1958. It was also fitted later with a 250cc engine, and set up a number of quarter-litre records as well.

Towards the end of the 1950s Moto Guzzi's design chief Giulio Carcano, accompanied by his assistant Emilio Cantoni, joined up with designer/motor-cyclist Gino Cavanna to build a record breaker around the pre-war supercharged 250cc single-cylinder engine. This engine, a one-off, had been fitted with a Cozette supercharger and was originally installed into a frame which ultimately went into production as the Condor and Albatros models. That machine had been ridden by the legendary Omobono Tenni to speeds of over 112mph. The same engine powered a post-war sidecar combination to 110mph, ridden by designer Cavanna, who took another highly streamlined combination to 138mph in 1952, beating previous records set by 500cc, 750cc and 1200cc machines.

Setting out for a new supercharged 250 four-wheeled record, using the blown 250 engine for power, Cavanna approached Ingegnere Barzocchi of Aeronautica Macchi to collaborate on the aerodynamics of the Cobra, a super-low-slung car with only just enough space between the rear wheels to allow it to be described as a four-wheeled vehicle. The rider lay on his stomach to keep the overall height, and thus the drag coefficient, as low as possible. The result was a number of new records, set on the Autostrada del Sole in May 1959, reaching a best speed of an incredible 145mph.

Then an Italian racing car maker called Stanguellini, a small company which had made something of a name for itself in Formula Junior racing, was persuaded by record contenders Campanella and Poggio to team up with the Modena firm of Gransport to build a fully enclosed streamlined car for an attack on a series of medium-distance quarter-litre records. The engine was a twin-cam single, coupled to a five-speed gearbox, and the driver sat centrally below an aircraft-type bubble canopy. Capable of speeds of up to 102mph, Colibri (Humming Bird), as the car was named, took the 50-to-200 Kilometre, the 50-to-100 Mile and One-Hour Class K International records.

Moto Guzzi's last involvement in four-wheeled vehicles actually resulted in the development of the 3 x 3 'Mechanical Mule'. The engine for that vehicle was designed by Giulio Carcano for a motor cycle application, but with the company running into difficulties, the idea of adapting it for car use came when the opportunity arose to supply Carcano's 500 V-twin as a power unit for the Fiat 500. Trials went so far as to adapt a Fiat gearbox to the Guzzi engine, but the 'Mechanical Mule' eventually became the final destination for the shaft-drive, Fiat-gearboxed engine, which became a 750 along the way. And that was the end of Mandello del Lario's involvement in four wheels.

The Stanguellini-Moto Guzzi 'Colibri'.

Moto Guzzi Models and Years of Build, 1920–2000

YEAR	MODEL	CC	YEAR	MODEL	CC
1920	Guzzi e Parodi	499cc	1974–1982	Nibbio	49cc
1921–1926	Normale	499cc	1975–1978	Le Mans 850	844cc
1923–1928	Sport	499cc	1975–1984	V1000 Convert	950cc
1923–1930	C2V Racer	499cc	1975–1987	850T3	844cc
1924–1933	C4V/ 4V TT/SS	499cc	1975–1987	T3 California	844cc
1926–1933	250TT/ SS	247cc	1976–1979	Magnum	49cc
1928–1930	Tipo 107 Motocarro	499cc	1977–1981	254	232cc
1928–1929	GT/GT16	499cc	1977–1986	V35/V35 II	346cc
1929–1930	Sport 14	499cc	1977–1986	V50/V50 II/V50 III	490cc
1930	Quattro Cilindri	492cc	1978–1981	Le Mans II	844cc
1931–1939	Sport 15	499cc	1978–1983	1000SP/1000NT	949cc
1930–1934	2VT/GT2VT	499cc	1978–1983	1000GS	949cc
1932–1936	Mototriclico 32	499cc	1979–1981	CX100	949cc
1932–1933	Tre Cilindri	492cc	1979–1981	125 2C4T	124cc
1932–1940	P175/P250 etc	175cc–247cc	1979–1984	V35 Imola	346cc
1933–1951	Bicilindrica Corsa	494cc	1979–1984	V50 Monza	490cc
1934–1948	V/GTV/GTW/GTC	499cc	1980–1983	850 T4	844cc
1934–1940	S/GTS	499cc	1980–1985	Le Mans III	844cc
1937–1940	PL/PLS/Ardetta/Egretta	247cc	1981–1987	California II	949cc
1938–1941	ER Motocarro	499cc	1982–1987	V65/V65SP	643cc
1938–1945	GT20/Alce	499cc	1982–1994	V35 Custom	346cc
1939–1940	Condor	499cc	1982–1994	V50 Custom	490cc
1939–1945	Albatros	247cc	1982–1994	V65 Florida	643cc
1939–1957	Airone/Airone Sport	247cc	1983–1985	850 T5	844cc
1940	Tre Cilindri	492cc	1984–1987	V35 TT	346cc
1942–1945	500U	499cc	1984–1987	V65 TT	643cc
1946	Edile	499cc	1984–1988	Le Mans IV	949cc
1946–1954	Motoleggera 65	65cc	1984–1988	1000SP II	949cc
1946–1951	Dondolino	499cc	1984–1989	V35 Imola II	346cc
1946–1951	Gambalunga	499cc	1984–1989	V50 Monza II	490cc
1946–1958	Super Alce	499cc	1984–1989	V65 Lario	643cc
1946–1980	Ercole Motocarro	499cc	1985–1988	C125 TT	123cc
1947–1948	250 Parallel Twin	247cc	1985–1990	V35 III	346cc
1949–1953	Astore	499cc	1985–1988	V75	744cc
1950–1967	Falcone	499cc	1986–1990	V35 NTX	346cc
1950–1966	Galletto	150cc–192cc	1986–1990	V65 NTX	643cc
1953–1966	Zigolo	98cc–110cc	1986–1990	V75 NTX	744cc
1954–1965	Cardellino	65cc–83cc	1987–1993	California III CI	949cc
1956–1966	Lodola	175cc–247cc	1987–1993	Mille GT	949cc

YEAR	MODEL	CC	YEAR	MODEL	CC
1956–1970	Ercolino Motocarro	192cc	1987–1995	350 GT	346cc
1960–1975	Stornello	125cc–160cc	1987–1995	650 GT	643cc
1961	3 x 3 Mule	754cc	1988–1992	SP III	949cc
1961–1963	Aiace Motocarro	110cc	1988–1993	Le Mans V	949cc
1961–1966	Motozappa	110cc	1989–1993	1000 S	949cc
1963–1976	Dingo	49cc	1989–1993	750 Targa	744cc
1965–1968	Dingotre	49cc	1989–1993	750 SP	744cc
1966–1973	Trotter	41cc–49cc	1989–1993	750 Strada	744cc
1967–1976	V7	704cc	1989–1997	350 Nevada	346cc
1968–1974	V7 Special/Ambassador	757cc	1989–1997	750 Nevada	744cc
1968–1974	V7 California	757cc	1991–1998	Daytona/RS	992cc
1968–1970	Ciclocarro Furghino	49cc	1992–1997	Quota 1000	949cc
1969–1976	Nuovo Falcone	499cc	1993	Strada 1000	949cc
1971–1975	850GT Eldorado/California	844cc	1993–2000+	California 1000EV	949cc
1971–1975	V7 Sport/750S/750S3	748cc	1993–2000+	California 1100	1064cc
1973–1975	850T	844cc	1994–1998	1000 Sport (IE)	949cc
1974–1976	Chiu	49cc	1994–1998	1100 Sport	1064cc
1974–1979	350GTS	346cc	1996–2000+	Centauro	992cc
1974–1979	400GTS	397cc	1996–2000+	Centauro GT	992cc
1974–1981	Tuttetereno	121cc	1996–2000+	Centauro Sport	992cc
1974–1982	250TS	231cc	1998–2000+	Quota 1100 ES	1064cc
1974–1982	Cross 50	49cc	1999–2000+	V11 Sport	1064cc

INDEX

Page numbers in *italics* indicate illustrations.